KEEP
LOVE

Also by Paul C. Brunson

*Find Love: How to Navigate Modern Love
and Discover the Right Partner for You*

KEEP
LOVE

21 TRUTHS FOR A
LONG-LASTING RELATIONSHIP

PAUL C. BRUNSON

flightbooks

Flight Books, part of Flight Studio, a Flight Group company

In collaboration with Ebury Publishing

UK | USA | Canada | Ireland | Australia
India | New Zealand | South Africa

Ebury Publishing is part of the Penguin Random House group of companies
whose addresses can be found at global.penguinrandomhouse.com

Penguin Random House UK
One Embassy Gardens, 8 Viaduct Gardens, London SW11 7BW

penguin.co.uk
global.penguinrandomhouse.com

Penguin
Random House
UK

flightbooks

First published by Ebury Publishing/Flight Books in 2025

1

Copyright © Paul C. Brunson 2025
Cowriter: Paul Murphy

The moral right of the author has been asserted.

Typeset by seagulls.net
Printed and bound in Great Britain by Clays Ltd, Elcograf S.p.A.

The authorised representative in the EEA is Penguin Random House Ireland,
Morrison Chambers, 32 Nassau Street, Dublin D02 YH68.

A CIP catalogue record for this book is available from the British Library

ISBN 9781785044694

Penguin Random House is committed to a sustainable future for our business, our readers and
our planet. This book is made from Forest Stewardship Council® certified paper.

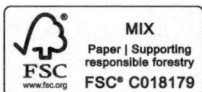

MIX
Paper | Supporting
responsible forestry
FSC
www.fsc.org
FSC® C018179

CONTENTS

INTRODUCTION

During my many years as a matchmaker, I was predominantly at the front end of the relationship continuum. My aim was to help people to recognise their skills and traits, what they needed to work on in themselves and how to identify the right partner. However, as the success of my and my wife Jill's matchmaking agency increased, and we were putting together more and more successful matches, our clients would turn around and say, 'I want to keep this person in my life. What do I do?' This was when I began to realise that there was very little reliable information available on how to sustain a relationship. This goes back to something I discussed in *Find Love*, the first book in this series — the study around relationships is still relatively new. The longest-running study of married couples is one conducted by a good friend of mine, Dr Terri Orbuch, and it's only been going since 1986.[1] Compared to other areas of psychological research, this is very little time at all.

So, when people asked for my advice about how to keep love, I had to respond based on what I knew from my marriage and the little I had picked up from what I'd read. This was when I realised that I needed to delve deeper to better understand why it can feel so hard to maintain a relationship and what goes into making the best ones work.

Find Love was all about choosing the best partner for long-term happiness. This book is for anyone who wants to keep love by sustaining a long-term partnership. That could be a marriage, or it could be that you're just cohabiting with someone. Or perhaps you're at an earlier stage of a committed relationship — you don't know if it's going to go for three months or thirty years, but you want to keep it. And not only do you want to keep it, but you want it to be more satisfying too. That's the key.

But even if you haven't identified that person and you're not yet in a relationship, there is still a lot of value in reading this book. Something I talked a lot about in *Find Love* was the idea that the best time to prepare for a relationship is before it begins. *Keep Love* will provide you with a master's degree in relationships, even if you're not yet in a partnership. It is therefore also great if you are single and looking for a committed relationship, as it provides a guide to understanding what is healthy in a relationship, what is not healthy, what you should be working towards and what tools and skills you could be developing that will be helpful now and in the future. In fact, the skills I discuss in this book can also be applied more widely in your life; they are not just applicable to your romantic relationships.

My ultimate aim, whatever your relationship status, is to increase your well-being as an individual. That's the best foundation for any strong relationship.

♥

Most of us consume our relationship insights from social media, television shows and digital platforms. But these forms of mass media mainly perpetuate dangerous myths about what is important when it comes to a successful relationship. This leads to a state of confusion that results in us seeking out and believing advice that is ultimately unhelpful. That's why I want to tackle these myths head-on and reveal the provocative truths about how to get the highest levels of satisfaction from your partnership.

I see these myths circulating all the time, whether it is on social media, or at a party, or at the barber shop, or when I'm on set filming *Married at First Sight* or *Celebs Go Dating*. In these circumstances, people tend to talk about their first-hand experiences, or the experiences of their friends. The information is not backed by research, which further entrenches the myths.

Instead, you need to inform yourself about the truth about relationships and develop the skills to make your partnership flourish and grow. This will help you to deal with the challenges that you will inevitably face. It is also important to equip yourself with the tools to manage those challenges, because when you look around the world, and especially in the UK and the USA, the average waiting time to see a therapist is six months to a year. Even if you have the means to go private, there is still a shortage of therapists, so you often end up on a waitlist anyway. And, in my experience, once you do get to see a therapist, satisfaction levels can be quite mixed. Most people don't go to therapy and then miraculously everything is rosy. Typically, you realise that the therapist is not the right person for you, so you stop seeing them and look for someone else. But there's a level of attrition that occurs, and many people never go back into the system, because they think therapy is just not for them. And then if you do go back into the system, you often start bouncing around. So, even though therapy can be incredibly beneficial, the initial challenge is to build a relationship and rapport with the right therapist before you can even get to the interventions. And that doesn't happen for most people.

There is no substitute for therapy, of course, but because it is not always a realistic option, you can think of this book as a complement to relationship therapy, outlining what you really need to know and a myriad of interventions that you can use to help you and your partner as you build a life together. And it will work regardless of whether your partner is willing to participate in the interventions or not. I see this book as being a dynamic tool that will not only help to save relationships that are perhaps floundering a bit, but will even more importantly help you to forge a more successful partnership, with strong levels of satisfaction.

I often hear people say that relationships require work, but they rarely talk about what that work actually entails. That's another reason why I wanted to write this book — to outline the work that is required to make a relationship the best it can be. Before my wife Jill and I got married, we were incredibly lucky to be able to do some premarital counselling. It was really a game-changer for us, because we were able to get a solid sense of the things we would need to work on and how to go about that right from the outset. The majority of couples don't have the benefit of someone providing them with those guidelines, which is where this book comes in. One of my main hopes is that you and your partner will read these topics, together or separately, and then simply have a discussion about them. But before you can even do that, it's about having the awareness that a healthy relationship takes work — everything always begins with awareness.

As well as explaining what really matters when it comes to relationships and why, I have also come up with a bespoke, self-guided exercise/intervention for every myth to help you put the truth into practice in your own partnership, and in life more generally.

Reading the book from cover to cover will give you a great understanding of what is important when it comes to a successful relationship. However, you can also use it more like a reference guide, dipping in and out to help you address any issues that might arise from time to time, and using the exercises to strengthen your relationship muscles. That said, a lot of the elements of advice in this book are linked to one another. It's therefore important that over time you attempt to develop the skills that pertain to all aspects of your relationship. Even if you're weaker in one of the areas, working across the board will see you rising with the tide and becoming stronger overall. Either way, I believe this is a book that every couple needs to have on their bookshelf.

♥

My qualifications to write this book are fourfold. One: my background and continuing work as a researcher, including for my podcast *We Need to Talk*, for which I've interviewed some of the foremost relationship experts in the world, such as Drs John and Julie Gottman, Gabor Maté, Dr Judith Joseph, Dr Tara Swart and Dr Terri Orbuch. Two: for the last fifteen years I've been commenting in the public forum on relationship trends, most of which turn out to be myths, and refuting them. Three: I am the co-owner of a therapy business with the psychologist Dr Angela Smith, who I have collaborated with extensively, benefiting from her years of experience in the process. This is important because, as I've explained, I see this book as a therapeutic tool. And four: after being matchmakers, Jill and I moved quite naturally into relationship coaching, specifically for people who were dating and not yet in serious relationships. Then, as our clients began to settle down and commit to a partner (or multiple partners, if that was their thing), we graduated to long-term relationship counselling and mentoring couples. Mentorship is something that is very popular in religious marital spaces, where you will be assigned a mentor from your church congregation by a pastor. But this type of mentorship is not confined to religious settings — it's something that we saw could be incredibly beneficial, and we have mentored couples at all stages of their relationships.

I have also been working as a relationship expert on TV for more than twelve years, and I have been happily married for more than twenty-two years. My work as the Global Relationship Insights Expert at Tinder has also allowed me access to a wealth of data and research. And I am asked to participate in research studies by corporate partners all the time. So, all in all, I spend a lot of time researching and learning about what makes couples tick and understanding how and why we stay together.

♥

My aim in this book is to outline all of the major issues and challenges that couples will go through in their partnerships and explain how you can manage them. That might be prevention, but no matter how much you anticipate and try to avoid disruption in your relationship, it will happen. And disruption can be good, as it allows you to acquire the tools to overcome it and come out stronger on the other end. My personal experience really supports this — following various disruptions in our marriage, Jill and I are in the strongest place we've ever been. I now want to share those tools with you so that you too can get the most out of your relationship and achieve the highest levels of well-being and satisfaction.

'IT'S SO INCREDIBLY
IMPORTANT TO HAVE
SOME OF YOUR EMOTIONAL
NEEDS MET BY A WIDE
RANGE OF PEOPLE OTHER
THAN YOUR PARTNER'

MYTH I

A GOOD PARTNER SHOULD FULFIL ALL YOUR NEEDS

*Provocative Truth: No partner can meet all your needs —
self-reliance and external support are essential*

Forming couples has always been a big feature of being human, but, as time has passed and society has changed, so too have partnerships. I have heard it said that, in the past, relationships were about money and the transfer of assets, but it's not really about that for most people these days — we now want more from our relationships. One of the main reasons for this, and something that I believe no one is really talking about when it comes to relationships, is how we've shifted from a collectivist to an individualist mindset in Western society.

Clovis I, the first king of the Franks and the godfather of modern-day France, converted to Christianity in 496 CE, leading to the widespread adoption of the religion among the previously pagan populations of what are today France, the Low Countries and Germany. That's what helped to spread the idea of marriage (the predominant form of relationship at that time), resulting in the development of townships based around nuclear families, as opposed to the clan structure that had come before. This led to the introduction of trade guilds, the creation of universities, a more complex hierarchy of organisation and governance, and greater efficiency. It was also the very beginning of the rise of individualism, with more value placed on being an individual as opposed to being part of the clan.

Over the centuries, this shift continued in the West, building through the Enlightenment period, the Industrial Revolution, the armed conflicts of the twentieth century and the growth of consumerism after the Second World War. In fact, you can track this trend right into the twenty-first century, with the COVID pandemic further cementing this sense of individualism. Many of us started to re-evaluate our lives and ask ourselves not 'Why are *we* here?' but 'Why am I here? What am I getting out of this world? I don't really like this job that I work all hours at. It's not good for my mental health. And it's not good for my physical health.'

In the process, we have gone from the lower echelons of Maslow's pyramid of fulfilling our basic needs towards the upper echelons and self-actualisation.[1]* And this has further magnified the focus on the self: 'I'm going to spend more time reading' or 'I'm going to spend more time identifying my passions' or 'I'm going to spend more time at the gym.' As a result of this self-development, we're now acquiring the tools and skills to interact with people more effectively.

As part of my role at Tinder, I wrote in *The Future of Dating Report 2023* that this is one of the reasons why some of us are going to have higher satisfaction in our relationships. But we're also going to have fewer relationships, because we will be so self-developed

---

* American psychologist Abraham Maslow proposed the idea of a pyramid of increasingly complex needs as you ascend, with physiological requirements (like food and shelter) at the bottom, followed by safety (such as good health and protection from danger), love and belongingness (including intimate relationships and friendships), self-esteem (for instance, respect and recognition), and self-actualisation (sometimes referred to as reaching your full potential).

that we're not willing to deal with mediocrity or what we perceive as someone who is toxic. The upside is that we can build stronger relationships. The downside to this is that we are now so focused on the self that there's more of a short-term perspective, there's less dedication, we're faster and it's all about the grass being greener on the other side. The moment someone chews with their mouth open, it's 'They're not for me. They gave me the ick.'

The rise in individualism has also seen an increase in loneliness and inequality. As a result, there's more division between people and in society more generally. It therefore makes sense that there are fewer partnerships, marriages and committed relationships now. But it also makes sense that the strongest marriages are stronger than ever before, because people have the tools to succeed.

An extension of this move towards individualism and the pursuit of self-actualisation is the increased focus on your partner to fulfil all of your needs, whether that be sex, security, companionship, intellectual stimulation or any of the myriad other things that we look for from other people. In the past, a partner only needed to fulfil a couple of your needs, but as society moved towards the nuclear family model and the elevation of the individual, more emphasis was placed on your partner being everything to you. This means we often focus solely on finding the perfect match, rather than considering our own growth.

Take, for example, the online dating world and dating apps, which promote the idea that you need to find 'the one', or the deluge of advertisements around Valentine's Day. Then there's social media, television and magazines, which all talk about finding the perfect partner, while also telling you that's what you deserve. *You are the best person in the world. You have no issues. Everyone else is toxic. Everyone else is a narcissist. You deserve the best of the best of the best. And you should never compromise, because 99 per cent is not enough when you deserve 100 per cent.* This is this whole machine that we're in right now. And the onus is on each of us to determine what we need ourselves. We don't have the same village to support us with such a momentous decision as choosing a long-term partner as we did in the past.

FALSE EXPECTATIONS

Having those heightened, unrealistic expectations about what a partner can give you can lead to you having more dependence upon them, placing unnecessary strain on the relationship. It can also lead to you — and I feel this has happened in my own life — neglecting other relationships, family members and friends. You end up disregarding all of these people in your life that you actually need for a well-rounded support system.

Unrealistic expectations that are never going to be met can also lead to disappointment and potentially resentment when your partner is not able to live up to the incredibly high standards that you're placing on them. And the data really bears this out. In order to get a sense of shifting trends, I compared the habits of married couples in the UK and the USA in the 1960s versus married couples today (the available data is on marriages, but it is just as applicable to any long-term relationship). Back then, married couples actually spent substantially less time one-on-one and spent more time as a family, with 85 per cent having family dinners together and regularly meeting up and going on outings with extended family, whereas it's less than 50 per cent today.[2] Additionally, when you adjust for inflation, married couples in the 1960s had less income, fewer assets and lower levels of education, which are all factors that many researchers today point to as being important when it comes to relationship success, as fewer financial pressures lead to less strain on the relationship in general. But despite the fact that couples spent less time together and had less financial security in the 1960s, marital satisfaction was much higher in the UK and the USA versus today.

In the 1960s, only 30 per cent of couples reported frequent, serious conflict in their relationship compared with 60 per cent today.[3] These conflicts include things like work—life balance, disputes over children and money, and the intrusion of technology. One theory why this is the case is that work and personal life were more distinct in the 1960s, and roles within the household were better defined, which speaks to an increased sense of perceived equity, although it's important to recognise that this so-called equity was often imbalanced, with women bearing the brunt of rigid gender roles, which likely suppressed their voices and contributed to less visible conflict. The deterioration of this separation over time has led to more stress and conflict. This touches upon the notion that we are everything to one another today, whereas there are benefits to finding your role and performing it well. This is the key to a successful team, for instance, but it applies to our relationships too. We can't do it all, and we can't expect someone to do it all for us either. Understanding what you can and cannot expect your partner to do for you leads to less stress and conflict, and a happier, healthier relationship.

I also looked at the divorce and separation rates in the 1960s compared with today. Women had fewer options and less agency back then when it came to being able to end a relationship (which, again, was usually a marriage), but that began to change with the introduction of the no-fault divorce in 1969 in the UK[4] and by Governor Ronald Reagan in California in the same year.[5] This led to an increase in the divorce rate in the UK and the USA, peaking in the 1990s, after which it has trended downwards, although levels are still higher today than in the 1960s.[6]

So, what are the reasons for this? Well, the one that seems most relevant to me is the idea that your partner can fulfil all of your needs — a standard that is so high that it is no surprise that we often fall short, leading to lower levels of satisfaction. We have unachievable requirements of our partners, and it's very hard to do anything about it. As soon as you suggest that someone doesn't place the same level of expectation on their partner, they inevitably say something like, 'Oh, so you're saying I should settle? You don't think I deserve 100 per cent?' And although I don't advocate that people should compromise what is truly important to them, I do think the ultimate answer is that we need to lower our expectations at least a little bit, because if 100 per cent is your minimum requirement, you have a higher probability of getting 100 per cent of nothing. I don't know of one high-satisfaction relationship in which both partners felt like they were getting 100 per cent on day one. I certainly don't think Jill thought she was getting someone who could meet 100 per cent of her needs when she married me.

In my previous book, *Find Love*, I said it is important to feel like you are choosing a partner, rather than being chosen by them. And I still stand by that. What I'm saying here is that you need to recalibrate your expectations about what your partner is going to deliver to you. You also need to let go of things that are inconsequential to the success of your relationship. The five fundamental qualities you should be looking for in a partner are: emotional fitness, courageous vision, resilient resourcefulness, open-minded understanding and compassionate support. These qualities then need to be underpinned by the right relationship dynamics: the same relationship goals, shared values, physical attractiveness/aligned sexual boundaries and genuine interest. This is what you really need in a partner for a successful relationship, and it does not include choosing someone who meets 100 per cent of your needs. Yes, you should have high standards, but you shouldn't have unrealistic expectations.

Instead, many of us focus on things that are ultimately unimportant. 'What is your star sign and what is your love language?'

I see these two things being talked about over 'What do you believe politically?' Over 'What was your first relationship like?' Over 'What does love mean to you?' Over 'What are your relationship goals?' Many of us make the most important decision of our lives based on the most inconsequential things. At the end of the day, it really doesn't matter what your star sign or your love language is, and it doesn't matter if some of your emotional needs are met by your friends and family instead of your partner. In fact, there are real benefits to drawing on a wide range of people for love and support.

WHAT DO WE NEED?

We need to use the right criteria, but we shouldn't be looking for someone who is 100 per cent perfect or who fulfils every need. In some ways, what you're looking for is someone who's also growing independently. So, they're not self-actualised any more than you are, but they're on the path towards that. After all, the journey is more important than the destination. And part of being on that journey is figuring out the things you need in life. Until that point, you just have a long list of wants, and you judge who to be with based on those wants, as opposed to a deeper exploration of what you need. I'd estimate that nine out of ten people I talk to don't really know what their values are, yet they're ready to wean people out of their life because they don't match them (see Chapter 13 for more on this).

We need to have a better understanding and definition of what our needs are in the first place. And I'm beginning to realise more and more that to do that requires us to face and overcome challenges in life. Start by reflecting on past experiences where you felt stretched or uncertain, as they often reveal your core needs. It's not as simple as sitting down and doing an exercise or meditating on it. Determining what your needs really are necessitates putting yourself in challenging, arduous situations so that you can then glean from them what it is that you actually need. We're more resilient, tougher and smarter than we know. And it's not until you're in the fire that you can learn what it is that you actually can do — and what you can't do, of course, because it's also important to identify the areas you are weak in and need help or inspiration or motivation with.

This is perhaps one of the reasons that I see empty nesters and people in middle age and beyond doing quite well in the dating market. About two years ago, a family friend of ours passed away and his wife was able to bounce back relatively quickly. You might have thought she would have found it difficult to meet new people, as she didn't fit the stereotypical profile of someone who does well on dating apps, for example. But the opposite was, in fact, true. She had no shortage of interest, and in a relatively short amount of time was able to meet someone with whom she wanted to be in a committed relationship. I think a large part of this was to do with the fact that she had been in challenging situations, especially with her husband, and come out the other side with so much clarity on life. Once you have been through something like that, you have less tolerance for nonsense, and you can pinpoint it more easily. In other words, you know what is important, and you know what you need. I think for all of us, living as much life as possible, as early as possible, is to our benefit when selecting a partner and sustaining a relationship.

OUTSIDE SUPPORT

A Michigan Institute study run by Dr Terri Orbuch found that having external sources of support and not relying solely on your spouse for emotional fulfilment is what contributes most to your relationship happiness and longevity.[7] Fostering self-reliance and building a diverse support network allows for the cultivation of healthier, more resilient, fulfilling relationships.

However, a lack of diversity in our support networks is where I think a lot of us fall short. As we get older, not only do our social circles shrink, they also have a tendency to look just like us. This leads to a reduction in the diversity of ideas and new information that we are subjected to, which, in turn, diminishes our ability to challenge fixed ideas and ignorance, stunting our growth. It's similar to why some people do crosswords or play chess — they're keeping their minds sharp. That's what having a diverse group of friends does to you. And that's why it's so incredibly important to have some of your emotional needs met by a wide range of people other than your partner.

The practical benefits of having that support network include a more balanced relationship with your significant other, because you are able to lean on outside opinions and perspectives, in much the same way as you can if you have a close friend who is someone with whom you could be romantically involved (we'll discuss this further in Chapter 15). It also promotes better personal growth, and one of Carol Ryff's six dimensions of well-being is around your personal connections, so it helps to boost overall well-being from that perspective too.[8]*

Relieving the burden on your partner to meet all of your needs because you're now tapping into other parts of your village reduces the pressure on them. It also builds resilience and helps you to cope better with challenges and setbacks as a result of having a strong support system. In his book *The Good Life*, Dr Robert Waldinger writes that you live longer, you're healthier,

---

* The six-factor model of psychological well-being developed by psychologist Carol Ryff is an assessment tool that measures six dimensions of well-being: autonomy, environmental mastery, personal growth, positive relations with others, purpose in life and self-acceptance. High scores in each of these areas points to someone who is psychologically healthy and leading a good life.

your system can fight off stress and you make more money, among other things, by having a strong partner, but also by having a diverse social network.[9]

You also get the benefit of having role models and mentors in your life who you can get advice from or look to emulate. And you get the similar benefit of passing on what you know to mentees, because they can also inspire you. The strongest circle is one that includes aspirational people. These are the mentors who've already done it and who you can learn from. Then you need the inspirational people, who tend to be your peers who are also trying to do it. And then you need the motivational people, who might not be attempting to do what you're doing, but who motivate you as a result of their efforts.

I know this is something that some people find easier than others, but, ultimately, if you can nurture a diverse social circle that can offer you support and meet some of your needs, that will be incredibly beneficial to your relationship. It's something I see lacking in the lives of many retired people, my own parents included. They cocoon themselves away from people and, because they're not working any more, they have no interactions outside of their relationships. The COVID pandemic was a hugely isolating experience for a lot of people, but my parents, who retired just before it started, didn't see much of a change in their day-to-day lives, as their interactions with other people were already so diminished. And I can see how that would weigh on all aspects of their lives. When they came to visit us in London recently, my father was interacting with people he didn't know for the first time in quite a while, and I could see that it energised him — he was excited to talk to new people. I would love to be able to help them replicate this in their daily lives. But it's much harder to create a social network after the fact — we should instead be cultivating those friendships throughout our entire lives if we can.

This applies especially to men, who are much less adept at consciously building their village over time. This does not necessarily mean that you need to actively identify the people you want in your life so you can lean on them for emotional support; it just requires you to do activities or events with these people and interact with them in a casual but frequent manner. We can use technology to help us to do this, and focusing on meeting new people related to something you are passionate about is also beneficial. My father did quite well in business, so perhaps he could be a mentor, which, as I mentioned, can be very enriching and rewarding.

It's about having the mindset that you are open to making new connections all the time and not being satisfied with only those you've already made, regardless of how strong those connections are. There is always room for more. As I discussed in *Find Love*, anthropologist Robin Dunbar has identified that, on average, people have approximately 150 people in their social circles, but contacts on the periphery drop off and new people join all the time.[10] This is where sociologist Mark Granovetter's concept of cultivating weak ties to strengthen and expand your network plays a part. In short, his theory is that the best opportunities come from people you don't know very well, as you are more likely to have exhausted the possibilities with the people you know well. It is therefore beneficial to look for and invite new connections, what he calls 'weak ties', into your network. It is also a good way of bringing diverse voices into your social circle, and therefore expanding the number of your needs that can be met outside your relationship.[11] After all, no one person can or should meet all of your needs, and self-reliance and external support are therefore essential if you want to have the best relationship possible.

SELF-GUIDED INTERVENTION: HAVING REALISTIC EXPECTATIONS IN RELATIONSHIPS AND UNDERSTANDING THE IMPORTANCE OF EXTERNAL SUPPORT

OBJECTIVE

To encourage you to release the unrealistic expectation that a partner should fulfil all of your needs, and to foster self-reliance and develop external support systems.

INTRODUCTION

There's a prevalent myth that a good partner should be able to meet all of your emotional, physical and intellectual needs. This belief, although romantic, places immense pressure on relationships and can lead to dissatisfaction. The reality is that no one person can, or should, fulfil every need of another. Instead, cultivating diverse sources of support — through friendships, family, hobbies and other relationships — can lead to healthier, more fulfilling partnerships. This intervention will help you to assess your expectations, understand what you truly need from a partner, cultivate a balanced and healthy dynamic by understanding the importance of diverse emotional support and personal growth, and explore ways to build a well-rounded support system.

PART I: UNDERSTANDING THE MYTH AND ITS IMPACT

I. RECOGNISE UNREALISTIC EXPECTATIONS

- Reflect by asking yourself if you have ever felt disappointed in your partner for not meeting a specific emotional or intellectual need, and how this affected your relationship.
- Unrealistic expectations can lead to frustration and dissatisfaction. Wanting your partner to fulfil all your emotional, sexual and intellectual needs is an immense and often impossible task for one person to take on.

- Example: 'I used to expect my partner to be interested in everything I cared about, from my work to my hobbies. But I realised that expectation created unnecessary tension and disappointment.'

2. IDENTIFY UNHEALTHY DEPENDENCY

- When you expect your partner to meet all your needs, it can lead to an unhealthy dependence, where you rely on them for every aspect of emotional support. If they are unable to meet these expectations, it often results in resentment.
- Example: 'I always relied on my partner for emotional validation, but when they were unavailable or didn't respond in the way I needed, I felt hurt. Over time, this created tension between us.'

3. THE HISTORICAL SHIFT TOWARDS INDIVIDUALISM

- Historically, relationships were more collective, with families and communities helping to meet various needs. Over time, the shift towards individualism in modern society has increased the pressure on romantic partners to fulfil all of our needs.
- Research insight: A study by Eli Finkel on 'suffocation marriages' reveals that as couples seek more emotional fulfilment from their spouses, there is often a sense of emotional suffocation when those expectations aren't met.[12] The idea of relying solely on one person is not sustainable for long-term happiness.

PART 2: RE-EVALUATING WHAT YOU TRULY NEED

I. DISTINGUISH BETWEEN WANTS AND NEEDS

- Reflect on what you expect from your partner. Are these essential needs or simply desires? Needs are non-negotiable aspects, such as emotional support or aligned life goals, while wants are preferences like shared hobbies or personality traits that might not be crucial for a successful relationship.

- Activity: Make a list of five things you expect from your partner and categorise them into 'Needs' versus 'Wants'.
- Example: 'I realised that while I want my partner to be as social as I am, it's not necessary for a happy relationship. What I really need is their emotional availability.'

2. DEFINE CORE NEEDS IN A RELATIONSHIP
- The five essential qualities to look for in a partner are:
  - **Emotional fitness:** Can they manage their emotions well?
  - **Courageous vision:** Do they have long-term goals and plans for the future?
  - **Resilient resourcefulness:** Can they handle challenges and setbacks?
  - **Open-minded understanding:** Are they open to new perspectives?
  - **Compassionate support:** Are they empathetic and supportive during difficult times?
- Reflect and ask yourself if your partner meets these core needs. If they don't, which areas could be improved or benefit from outside support?
- Example: 'While my partner doesn't share my love of intellectual debates, they are deeply compassionate, which is more important in the long run.'

PART 3: BUILDING A DIVERSE SUPPORT SYSTEM
I. UNDERSTAND THE IMPORTANCE OF EXTERNAL RELATIONSHIPS
- Having a network of friends, family and mentors can take the pressure off your romantic relationship. Research by Dr Terri Orbuch shows that relying on multiple sources for emotional fulfilment leads to stronger relationships and greater personal well-being.
- Example: 'I used to feel like I needed my partner's attention all the time, but when I reconnected with my friends, I realised

they could fulfil some of my need for social interaction and fun.'

2. EXPAND YOUR SOCIAL CIRCLE

- Action step: Reflect on the current diversity of your social circle. Does it include a variety of people with different perspectives and experiences? If not, look for ways to expand it through activities or shared interests.
- Example: 'After joining a local book club, I found new friends who could provide intellectual stimulation, freeing my partner from feeling obligated to engage in conversations they weren't interested in.'

3. IDENTIFY MENTORS AND PEERS

- Find mentors who can offer wisdom and guidance, and peers who are on a similar journey. Surrounding yourself with people who challenge and inspire you outside of your relationship will enhance your personal growth and your relationship.
- Example: 'I started seeking advice from a mentor in my industry. It helped me grow professionally and gave me a new perspective on my relationship.'

PART 4: STRENGTHENING THE RELATIONSHIP THROUGH BALANCED EXPECTATIONS

I. DISCUSS EXPECTATIONS WITH YOUR PARTNER

- Open a dialogue with your partner about realistic expectations. Talk about what you each need from the relationship and how external support systems can help you both to feel more balanced.
- Conversation starter: 'I've realised that I've been expecting you to meet all of my emotional needs, and I think that's been putting too much pressure on our relationship. Let's talk about what we both need and how we can support each other while also finding other ways to feel fulfilled.'

- Example: 'We agreed that it's OK to turn to friends and family for certain types of support. It's taken some of the pressure off and improved our communication.'

2. CELEBRATE INDIVIDUAL GROWTH

- Encourage one another to pursue personal interests and passions. These pursuits bring not only fulfilment but also new energy into the relationship. Independence leads to more satisfaction, and research shows that partners who encourage each other's growth report higher levels of relationship happiness.
- Example: 'My partner encouraged me to start my own business, which helped me to feel more fulfilled. Now, I bring that sense of achievement into our relationship.'

3. DEFINE SHARED GOALS AND INDIVIDUAL PURSUITS

- Activity: Create two lists with your partner: one for shared goals and one for individual pursuits. Having clear goals helps align your relationship, while individual pursuits maintain independence and personal growth.
- Example: 'We decided that travelling together is a shared goal, but we also have our own hobbies — my partner enjoys painting, while I love running marathons.'

CONCLUSION

No partner can fulfil all of your needs, and expecting them to do so leads to frustration and dissatisfaction. By building a strong support network and pursuing individual growth, you can reduce the pressure on your relationship and foster a deeper, more meaningful connection with your partner.

THE INTERVENTION IN PRACTICE

Jill and I have talked quite a bit about the fact that moving to the UK was the best thing we ever did for our well-being. This surprises a lot of people, either because they don't know much about the UK and don't think it is a good place to live or, and this is more common, because they thought we would suffer from being apart from our friends and family. But the fact is that it forced us to find new, diverse social circles, and it pushed us to learn new things outside of our comfort zone in Washington, DC. And we didn't really leave our social network behind. We can still lean on them from afar. We've instead increased our opportunities to meet new people and, by doing so, have expanded our social network. It's also given us the chance to connect with extended family. I have cousins in West London who I've been able to reconnect with, and a cousin who lives in Amsterdam who I have now met for the first time, there and here in the UK. These are people who I have a new connection with that widens the horizon of my world, which in turn provides me with more people I can interact with to fulfil my many needs beyond Jill and my boys.

TAKEAWAY

Fulfilling relationships are built on balanced expectations, self-reliance and strong external support systems. Cultivate independence, expand your social circles and allow your partner to focus on the qualities that truly matter, instead of expecting them to meet all of your emotional, physical and intellectual needs.

'A RELATIONSHIP WITH NO
CONFLICT IN IT WILL NOT BE
AS STRONG AS ONE IN WHICH
A COUPLE ADDRESSES AND
OVERCOMES CONFLICT IN
A HEALTHY WAY'

MYTH 2

AVOIDING CONFLICT PRESERVES PEACE IN RELATIONSHIPS

*Provocative Truth: Constructive conflict can
strengthen relationships by improving
communication and understanding*

There is a widespread belief that when you avoid conflict, it's actually helpful to your relationship, because conflict is bad. Even the most astute people will often resort to saying, 'Let's just not fight. Let's keep the peace.' I hear this sort of thing all the time on the dating shows I work on, in messages that are sent to me and in my matchmaking work: 'Our relationship is terrible because we argue all the time.' The inverse implication of this is: 'If we didn't argue all the time, our relationship would be great.' And while it is true that constant arguing does not make for a healthy or enjoyable relationship, it's not really the arguments that are bad. It's the inability to resolve the conflict that is the problem. You need to have the skills to navigate disagreements, but you can't create the skills you need to resolve those disagreements unless you have conflict in the first place.

One of the most interesting things to me about this particular myth is that it persists all over the world — in the East and West, among every culture and socio-economic group, which makes it somewhat unique. And I believe people fall into the trap of believing it to be true for three main reasons, the first of which is societal and cultural norms. In East Asian culture, for example, the predominant philosophy is that arguing and rifts are bad and peace and tranquillity are good. Then, if you consider the workplace, arguments or disagreements are again perceived to be counterproductive. If there's any type of disagreement, what typically happens is you see the people go into an office and close the door so no one else can hear.

Television and film also play a huge role in the concept that conflict is something to be avoided. If you think about *Married at First Sight*, or even *Celebs Go Dating*, the point of view that is most often put across is that when there's conflict, there's drama, and then there's pain, which is to be avoided at all costs. On *Married at First Sight UK*, for example, couples often retreat into silence or surface-level politeness when they encounter issues, preferring to maintain a sense of harmony rather than risk the discomfort of open confrontation. This leads to suppressed emotions that eventually manifest in other ways. Similarly, on *Celebs Go Dating*, you frequently see participants opting to 'brush things under the rug' when confronted with incompatibilities or misunderstandings, choosing instead to play along to avoid rocking the boat or facing the possibility of being perceived negatively. This perpetuates the idea that maintaining a facade of calm, even at the expense of authenticity, is more desirable than engaging in the difficult but potentially growth-promoting conversations that real conflict might bring.

On the flip side, the critically acclaimed film *Marriage Story* with Scarlett Johansson and Adam Driver offers a rare example of what really happens when a couple attempts to avoid conflict. In the film, they have decided to divorce, but they choose not to engage in conflict or argue while doing so because they want to protect their child and think it will lead to a more peaceful and amicable separation for them and the people around them. This is an understandable point of view, but not addressing the issues between them ends up being even more deleterious to their relationship.

When it comes to the cultural norms around this subject, the patriarchy still rears its head. Growing up, if I got into trouble at school, when I got home my mother would always say, 'We'll wait until your dad gets home. He's going to handle this.' I hate to call her out for that, but those attempts at avoiding conflict and keeping the peace were not a great example to set. You often see this happen on television. My family and I binge-watched *Young Sheldon*, and his mum would similarly tell him, 'Wait until your father gets home. He's gonna handle this.' It's a way of deferring the potential stress and anxiety that comes with the conflict and avoiding the friction.

Learned behaviour is also a factor. If you were brought up in a family where your parents tried to hide conflict from you, then that's something you might think is normal. In the past, when people married for pragmatic reasons in order to fulfil the more basic needs towards the bottom of Maslow's hierarchy of needs (see page 10), there was less reason to engage your partner in conflict. You weren't sharing your whole life with your partner; you were only sharing one or two facets of it. The goal wasn't self-actualisation. Today, as we explored in the last chapter, more of us want to be self-evolved and to reach our full potential, meaning that we want more from our partners. This means there is more opportunity for conflict, as the stakes are higher, and you also need conflict in order to stimulate growth, so it is necessary if you want to have the strongest relationship. But because the stakes were lower in previous generations and the norm was to avoid conflict, this behaviour can be passed down from parents to their children.

The third factor, as suggested by the characters in *Marriage Story* attempting to keep the peace, is the fear of some type of negative outcome from conflict; for example, that you're going to become emotionally hurt or you're going to have to emotionally hurt someone else, and you don't want to be hurt or hurt the people you love. Or perhaps you fear that conflict could actually cause your relationship to break up, so you instead choose to live in a place of mediocrity and not being satisfied just so that you can keep the fumes of the relationship going, as opposed to being engaged in a relationship where there's fire and passion.

The fourth reason is that we generally lack the skills to negotiate and overcome conflict successfully, so we decide to not engage with it instead. And this is a big issue that I have with education systems around the world: they are not equipping our young people to be able to actively listen, resolve conflict or exhibit emotional intelligence. In fact, we are not teaching people the skills to identify that there is a problem in the first place, let alone to investigate or analyse that problem. As a result, we definitely don't have the skills to resolve those problems.

THE DOWNSIDES TO AVOIDING CONFLICT

If you avoid conflict, it can be detrimental to your relationship in two main ways.

POOR COMMUNICATION

Communication is the lifeblood of any relationship. Like Michelangelo sculpting a block of marble to reveal the masterpiece within, your partner is helping to chip away to unveil the beautiful, self-evolved being that you are, and communication is their hammer and chisel. Without this communication, you are left with lots of unresolved problems.

Couples rarely split up because of one thing; instead, it's more often than not death by a thousand cuts. When you're not resolving conflict, it allows those small hairline fractures to persist and worsen.

LACK OF EMOTIONAL INTIMACY

In order to reach the highest level of satisfaction in your relationship, you need to reach a place of strong emotional connection. And the only way to get that emotional connection is to go through friction. Dr Angela Smith says we all have a public life, a private life and a secret life. In order to access your partner's secret life, you have to hear a lot of uncomfortable truths, and you have to be able to overcome your biases and preconceived ideas. Only then can you get to that place of strong emotional connection. If you're not resolving conflict, you'll never get there.

Overall, you will have lower satisfaction with the relationship, which can spill over into all aspects of your life. There is a domino effect that can be very significant — meaning that you make less money and are less satisfied at work, you have higher stress levels, and lower levels of physical and mental well-being.

THE POWER OF CONFLICT

The best analogy I've heard for the power of conflict is likening it to muscle growth. In order to encourage hypertrophy, you have to put pressure on your muscles and break them down. Then, with rest and the right nutrition, the muscles grow back stronger. With conflict in your relationship, it's the same thing. The conflict is the stress, and the skills you use to overcome and navigate conflict are what help your relationship to grow. So, ultimately, you can only grow your relationship, and you can only be highly satisfied in it, if you are resolving disagreements, and that means you have to go through conflict. Perhaps somewhat counter-intuitively, a relationship with no conflict in it will not be as strong as one in which a couple addresses and overcomes conflict in a healthy way.

This means that when conflict arises, you should not avoid it, because you're only going to store up problems for further down the line — when I interviewed Drs John and Julie Gottman for my podcast, they told me that '69 per cent of conflict will not be resolved in the relationship'. I would therefore go even further and say you need to seek out conflict if you want to grow as an individual and as a couple.

DEVELOPING THE SKILLS

Reading Sun Tzu's *The Art of War* was a game-changer for me. He said that the most successful generals spend more time off the battlefield preparing for war than they do on it. The same is true when it comes to dealing with relationship conflict — developing the skills is the key piece of the puzzle. And developing those skills will help you in every aspect of your life. As I said before, it's so important that I think it's something we should be teaching our children in schools, starting with the following.

ACTIVE LISTENING

This skill is probably at the top of the list when it comes to those needed to overcome conflict successfully. Active listening is not just sound hitting your eardrums — there needs to be some kind of conscious evaluation of those sounds, and some sort of action as a consequence. Maybe the action is a value-added statement. For example, in a conversation in which your partner shares their stress about work, you might respond with, 'It sounds like you're feeling overwhelmed by everything on your plate — how can we tackle this together to make things feel more manageable?' Maybe it is that you've acknowledged what the other person has said and internalised it so that it can help you out in a similar situation in the future. Whatever the action is, the important thing is that you don't just listen to the sounds the other person is making; you need to really hear what they are saying and act upon it.

It sounds so simple when you explain it like that, but I truly believe most people don't engage in active listening very often. I see it with my kids all the time. I tell them something and realise they are not really listening to me. With my eldest son in particular, I can see in his eyes that he's just waiting to respond: 'Dad's on his soapbox again. I'm just going to wait for him to stop talking, and then I'm going to say what I want to say.' This is not a good strategy if you want to confront conflict successfully.

BODY LANGUAGE

I truly believe it when body language expert Janine Driver says that our bodies say more than our words. The problem is, many of us misinterpret body language. I was recently speaking to someone who interviews people for a living and is extremely astute. She said to me that when a guest comes in with their arms folded, she immediately knows that they're going to be confrontational. But that's not necessarily what folded arms mean. It could mean that, of course, but you can't know for sure until you have benchmarked the person. Maybe they're just comfortable folding their arms, which enables them to articulate themselves better, or maybe they're just cold. There are a myriad of reasons why someone would exhibit any given gesture or pose, which is why it is essential to actively develop observation skills, such as paying attention to subtle changes in posture and expression, so you can interpret body language in the moment and on a case-by-case basis. If you embrace conflict within your relationship, you will come to recognise what your partner's body language is telling you over time.

I became adept at interpreting body language by reading every book out there on the subject, by experts such as Janine Driver and Joe Navarro, and I've been to seminars and workshops to help enhance my skills. Being a matchmaker and working closely with people has also been beneficial. Doing large speed-dating events all over the United States was particularly helpful, as they allowed me to observe people closely in an environment where they had their guard down. People-watching is also one of my favourite things to do. Jill and I love travelling to new places and sitting at an outdoor café, having a coffee and just looking at people and how they engage. And this hints at something that is important when it comes to developing your ability to read body language: you need to observe people outside of your own social circle and engage with the widest range of people as possible.

'I' STATEMENTS

If you've engaged in active listening and have heard what someone is actually trying to say, and if you've observed and understood someone's body language, the next step is to think about how you deliver what you want to say. In other words, how can you get across your point of view and actually have the other person receive it and not be defensive, or dismissive, or disrespectful? A lot of that, I believe, comes from understanding how to construct your communication. Simply removing the word 'you' and replacing it with 'I' is one extremely powerful way to do this. 'You did this' or 'you did that' inevitably puts your partner on the defensive, whereas 'I feel this way' moves them into a space of listening to and hopefully empathising with you.

CHOOSING A TIME AND A PLACE

Confronting conflict in the heat of the moment is not usually a good idea (more of which in Chapter 7), but just as important as *when* you talk about something is *where* you talk about it. Whether you attempt to resolve an argument in your house or on the walk to the coffee shop can really make the difference between the conflict being beneficial or detrimental.

Typically, people wait to resolve conflict at home. Perhaps a couple are at a dinner party when something happens and one of them says, 'Let's not talk about it now. We can handle this when we get home.' However, home is often the worst place to resolve conflict, because, for many people, it is where unresolved or toxic conflict has occurred in the past. Yes, home is a safe haven for many of us, but that's not the case for everyone. In fact, we know that couple satisfaction is declining over time,[1] so it follows that many are living in a place of dispute. For those people, home is not a neutral, fair zone. 'It's where I was yelled at.' 'It's where I was hit.' 'It's where I was treated unfairly.'

One study showed that removing yourself from the home and attempting to address a conflict outside or in a place that you feel is neutral, safe and fair is key to solving it successfully.[2] This is also why a lot of people wait to go to their therapist to address conflict. They are able to raise things with their partner in therapy because they feel they are in a safe environment. So, the context in which conflict takes place is extremely important, even to the point that your physical positioning is relevant. A head-on approach is confrontational to many people, especially men, so try not to face off when having a difficult conversation. Sitting across from one another at the kitchen table and looking one another in the eye is probably not the best way to go. You're setting yourself up for a confrontation rather than a resolution. Alternatively, on a walk, you're side by side. You're a team. The simple positioning of your bodies plays a big role in keeping things on an even keel.

♥

Although the myth that avoiding conflict preserves peace in a relationship does on the face of it seem logical, the truth is that conflict is inevitable and should be embraced, as it allows you to grow as a couple. If you try to avoid conflict at all costs, particularly the day-to-day disagreements, you will not be so well equipped to deal with the big challenges when they arise. That's why it is so important to develop conflict resolution skills.

SELF-GUIDED INTERVENTION: BUILDING CONFLICT RESOLUTION SKILLS THROUGH PRACTICAL ACTIVITIES

OBJECTIVE

To develop conflict resolution skills and embrace constructive conflict as a positive force in your relationship by engaging in new activities, practising mindfulness and holding regular 'state-of-the-union' meetings.

INTRODUCTION

Conflict is a natural part of any relationship, and learning to navigate it effectively can lead to stronger, more resilient partnerships. This intervention offers three practical ways to build the skills needed for constructive conflict resolution: engaging in new activities together, practising mindfulness and holding regular, focused discussions.

PART I: DOING NEW ACTIVITIES TOGETHER
I. UNDERSTAND THE CONCEPT

- Engaging in new, unfamiliar activities with your partner creates opportunities for disagreement and negotiation, helping you to practise conflict resolution in a controlled environment.
- These experiences can involve low-level conflicts, such as frustration or differing opinions, which provide valuable lessons in compromise, active listening and communication.

2. CHOOSE A NEW ACTIVITY

- Select an activity that neither you nor your partner has tried before. This could be a creative project (such as pottery), a physical challenge (such as rock climbing) or a collaborative game (such as board games or puzzles).
- The key is that the activity should be unfamiliar and require cooperation.

3. EMBRACE LOW-LEVEL CONFLICT

- As you engage in the activity, recognise moments of frustration, disagreement or miscommunication as opportunities to practise conflict resolution.
- Example: If you're struggling with a task during the activity, allow your partner to guide or assist you, and practise patience and active listening.

4. REFLECT AND COMMUNICATE

- After the activity, reflect on the experience together. Discuss what challenges arose and how you navigated them as a team.
- This process helps build a foundation for resolving more significant conflicts in the future.

PART 2: BEING IN THE MOMENT TOGETHER

I. UNDERSTAND THE CONCEPT

- Practising mindfulness together, by doing things like yoga or meditation, fosters a sense of calm and presence that can enhance your ability to handle conflict.
- Many couples feel uncomfortable sitting in silence, but embracing stillness together can help build comfort in each other's presence, even during challenging conversations.

2. PRACTISE MINDFUL ACTIVITIES

- Choose an activity like yoga, meditation or deep breathing exercises to practise together. The goal is to be still and in the moment with your partner, focusing on breath and awareness.

- If yoga isn't your preference, simply sitting together in a quiet space and focusing on your breath can be equally effective.

3. EMBRACE SILENCE

- Practise being comfortable in silence with your partner, whether at home or in public. Avoid the temptation to fill quiet moments with conversation or distractions like your phone.
- Over time, this practice will help you both feel more at ease during tense or emotionally charged moments in your relationship.

4. APPLY MINDFULNESS TO CONFLICT

- When conflict arises, draw on the mindfulness techniques you've practised together to stay calm and present. Focus on listening without reacting immediately, and use breathing exercises to stay grounded.

PART 3: STATE-OF-THE-UNION MEETINGS

I. UNDERSTAND THE CONCEPT

- A 'state-of-the-union' meeting is a dedicated time for you and your partner to address specific topics or issues. These meetings provide a structured way to discuss conflicts or concerns before they escalate.
- Psychologist John Gottman popularised this concept as a way to foster intentional communication.

2. SCHEDULE A MEETING

- Set aside time for a state-of-the-union meeting with your partner. This can be scheduled regularly (for example, weekly or monthly) or initiated when one of you feels the need to discuss a specific topic.

- Example: 'Do you have ten minutes to talk about something? Let's have a quick state-of-the-union meeting.'

3. ESTABLISH GROUND RULES
- Ensure that both of you are fully present: phones down, TV off and no distractions.
- Focus on one topic at a time. Each partner should have the opportunity to speak and be heard without interruption.
- Approach the conversation with empathy and a desire to resolve the issue constructively.

4. CONDUCT THE MEETING
- Begin the meeting by each expressing your thoughts and feelings on the chosen topic. Use 'I' statements to avoid placing blame.
- Actively listen to your partner's perspective and engage in a calm, solution-oriented dialogue.
- Example: 'I've been feeling overwhelmed with our schedule lately. Can we discuss ways to balance our time better?'

5. REFLECT AND FOLLOW UP
- After the meeting, reflect on how the conversation went. Did both of you feel heard? Were you able to reach a resolution?
- If necessary, schedule a follow-up meeting to revisit the topic or discuss progress.

CONCLUSION

By engaging in new activities, practising mindfulness and holding state-of-the-union meetings, you can build the skills needed to navigate conflict constructively. These self-guided interventions provide practical ways to enhance communication, foster emotional resilience and embrace conflict as an opportunity for growth.

THE INTERVENTION IN PRACTICE

Jill and I did pottery together for the first time. I thought I was going to be great at it, but I actually sucked. For whatever reason, I just couldn't seem to get my thumb in the correct position to control the clay on the wheel. I was getting a bit frustrated, and Jill repeatedly had to come over and help me. Although it might seem innocuous, that situation was one of low-level conflict. We sometimes think that conflict means the most severe and heightened interactions, but it can also be situations where there's just a little bit of friction. Me getting annoyed at the clay shooting everywhere was a minor conflict situation. Jill having to show me what to do demonstrated to me that it's OK to not know how to do something and to require help, and it showed Jill that she could approach me at a time when I might seem unapproachable. I was learning how to actively listen to her and take instruction, and she was learning how to deliver that instruction. Now, if something more challenging or serious happens in the future, we've already built the foundations for how to communicate in a moment of conflict.

Playing games can also function in a similar way. Jill and I play a *New York Times* game with our eldest son in which you have to find the themes that connect groups of words, similar to the connecting wall on the BBC TV programme *Only Connect*. There are inevitably disagreements about what the answers are, which leads to discussion and negotiation. This sort of conflict is inconsequential, but we are learning skills regardless. And when you are engaging in these lower levels of conflict and you resolve them, it gives you confidence to tackle the bigger things.

When it comes to state-of-the-union meetings, Jill and I have reached the point where our meetings aren't formally scheduled. Instead, one of us might say to the other, 'Hey, do you have ten minutes to talk about something?' And we know the rules so well by now that we don't have to set them out. In this way, we can avoid minor conflicts escalating.

TAKEAWAY

Conflict doesn't have to be destructive. By engaging in new activities, practising mindfulness and holding regular 'state-of-the-union' meetings, you can strengthen your ability to handle disagreements with confidence and compassion, ultimately strengthening your relationship's foundation.

'YOU FIRST HAVE TO REALISE THAT ROMANTIC LOVE IS CONDITIONAL, AND YOU THEN HAVE TO ACCEPT THAT SATISFACTION IS THE GOAL, NOT LONGEVITY'

MYTH 3

TRUE LOVE IS UNCONDITIONAL

Provocative Truth: Romantic love has conditions and endures because of mutual effort and agreed boundaries

The myth of love having no conditions rests on the idea that once two people fall in love, the bond should be unbreakable. In this conception of love, it is selfless, enduring and unwavering, regardless of circumstances or actions, able to withstand any challenge or limitation without exception.

I recently did a social media poll on this, and the majority of respondents said that true love is unconditional. I think this is probably true for some forms of love, particularly the love of a parent for a child. There may, of course, be extreme circumstances in which this unconditional love is tested to the maximum, but my guess is that even parents of children who do terrible things still love them. So, when I looked at this myth, I looked at it from the perspective of romantic love only.

One of the main sources of this idea comes from religious teachings around forgiveness and love being selfless because true love mirrors divine love, and divine love is unconditional. This is then magnified by culture and societal expectations, which are built around a human desire for security and permanence in a relationship, and a very comforting, idealistic view of love. This is very important, because most of us, I think, are ultimately seeking safety in our relationships, and knowing that your partner is going to love you unconditionally creates an overpowering feeling of safety.

I think we see this idea play out most often in popular music. There are so many songs that say that, no matter what you do to me or what happens, I'm going to be here for you, whether it is Whitney Houston's 'I Will Always Love You' or Adele's 'Someone Like You', both of which basically say that they will still love their partners even though they have moved on, or 'You Owe Me Nothing in Return' by Alanis Morissette, the title of which says it all. Songs like this suggest that love is unwavering and forever, regardless of what might happen in the relationship or what boundaries are crossed.

BELIEVING TRUE LOVE TO BE UNCONDITIONAL IS UNHEALTHY

The downsides to believing in love being unconditional include having unrealistic expectations about what love is. This can prevent you from finding it in the first place, because you feel like it is unattainable, leaving you always disappointed and frustrated. No relationship can ever measure up to those expectations. Next, it can lead to you tolerating harmful and toxic behaviour, because it could encourage you to stay in an unhealthy and perhaps even abusive relationship if you think true love is about enduring hardships. It can also cause you to neglect self-care if you always prioritise your partner's needs over your own well-being, thinking that true love means having to sacrifice for your partner. And, finally, it can lead to a lack of growth, because without recognising that there are conditions that need to be met and efforts that need to be made in a healthy relationship, partners will not do the necessary work to improve it.

There are countless studies that support the idea that love is, in fact, conditional, including a John Gottman and Robert Levenson five-year prospective study predicting divorce among newlyweds from 1992.[1]* Gottman also came up with the idea of the 'Four Horsemen' of negative behaviours that lead to ineffective conflict resolution and therefore the break-up of a relationship: criticism, defensiveness, stonewalling and contempt.[2] The research showed that if these things happened early in a relationship, there was a significant chance of dissolution, such that Gottman and his colleagues were able to develop a model whereby they could predict with 94 per cent accuracy which marriages would end in divorce.

The reason why this is important in terms of looking at conditional love is that it shows that successful relationships do, in fact, have some key conditions: one, you have to be able to resolve conflict in your relationship; and two, you need positive interactions. If you don't have those two things, the likelihood is that you will break up.

Another study by Ted Huston tracking 168 couples over thirteen years found that 54 per cent remained happily married after the study period concluded.[3] The marriages that thrived did so when partners continually met each other's emotional needs and adapted to any changes that were happening in the relationship. This showed that meeting your partner's emotional needs is another fundamental condition to a successful relationship.

A Pew Research survey on marriage and cohabitation in the USA in 2019 showed that 88 per cent of married adults cited love as a key reason for getting and staying married.[4] At the same time, 81 per cent cited companionship, 76 per cent cited commitment and 28 per cent cited financial stability, which shows that there

---

* Most of the formal research on relationships focuses on marriage, but the findings are applicable to all serious, committed relationships.

are many other conditions that go towards determining if you enter a relationship in the first place, and then if you decide to stay in it.

The 'State of Our Unions' by the conservative National Marriage Project in the USA conducted a survey that showed that 70 per cent of respondents believed that shared values and mutual respect were crucial for a successful marriage, and 65 per cent of respondents who were unhappily married cited a lack of emotional support and communication as primary issues, once again emphasising that respect, communication and shared values are key.[5]

The overall point I am making is that whenever a psychologist looks at what sustains a relationship, they identify a number of factors, and those factors, I would argue, are conditions.

THE KEY CONDITIONS OF LOVE

Based on the research and my own experience, I believe some of the key fundamental conditions of love to be as follows:

1. Emotional support and communication
2. Mutual respect
3. Equitable division of household labour
4. Financial stability and responsibility
5. Commitment and effort
6. Adaptability and growth

One of the main tools available to researchers when assessing a qualitative experience such as relationship satisfaction is a self-report questionnaire graded on a scale. Specifically in the study of relationships, many researchers have employed variations of what are known as marital-adjustment scales. These scales measure a person's ability to adapt or adjust to changes and challenges within their relationship. This adaptability is, in my view, one of the most essential conditions of love. Without it, maintaining a successful relationship becomes significantly more difficult. For instance, imagine a couple facing a major life transition, like one partner losing their job. If both partners can react to this setback by adjusting their expectations, roles and even their lifestyle to accommodate the new reality, they are demonstrating the flexibility and resilience that sustain long-term love. They might support one another emotionally, create new routines or even take on temporary roles they hadn't before. This ability to shift and adapt not only stabilises the relationship but strengthens the bond as the couple navigate the challenge together. Without this capacity, even the smallest disruptions can become insurmountable, leading to resentment and distance.

One study found that couples who demonstrate the ability to grow in their relationship are the most likely to experience high satisfaction, because couples who can adjust their behaviours and expectations over time show higher stability and satisfaction.[6]

From my perspective, you first have to realise that romantic love is conditional, and you then have to accept that satisfaction is the goal, not longevity (more of which in Chapter 21). The reason for this is because if you are just aiming for your relationship to last a long time, it can be without conditions. But if it's satisfaction that you're aiming for, it requires a variety of conditions, the primary one being our ability to adjust or adapt.

A FALSE DEFINITION OF LOVE

In some situations, the relationship could be in a poor state because of the actions of one of the partners, and the put-upon person could still say that they love their partner regardless. You might therefore argue that love is not conditional — yes, there are some conditions that if not met should lead to the end of a relationship, but that doesn't mean you have necessarily stopped loving the person. The problem with this, in my opinion, is that it rests on a false definition of what love really is. If someone is treating you badly, and the conditions for a high-satisfaction relationship are not being met, I'd argue that you are more likely in thrall to that person or infatuated with them than truly in love with them. Think of it this way: if love is made up of intimacy, commitment and passion, as defined by Robert Sternberg, and you are in a bad or even abusive relationship, I would argue that you don't love your partner based on that definition, because I don't believe it's possible to have a high level of emotional intimacy with someone who's treating you badly, for example.[7] In order to have love as defined by Sternberg, certain conditions must be met.

I have a somewhat morbid example that speaks to this: men leaving their wives who are terminally ill. A cancer research study conducted by the University of Utah School of Medicine showed that when you have an opposite-sex couple, regardless of how long they've been together or how happy they are — they can have been together for thirty years and report high marital satisfaction — and the man becomes terminally ill and the wife becomes the caretaker, there is a 2.9 per cent separation rate. So, basically, if you are a man and you become terminally ill, you are locked in — your partner is almost never going to leave you. But when you switch it around and it is the woman who's terminally ill, the separation rate climbs to 21 per cent.[8] This screams to me how conditional love actually is, because the moment that the need to caretake breaks your expectations, the moment that you're no longer getting emotional or practical support back, or sex is not happening, or whatever other condition you feel is not being met, that's it — it could be over.

ESTABLISHING THE CONDITIONS
THAT MATTER TO YOU

Recognising that there are conditions and knowing them up front, ideally when you are selecting a partner, helps across the board, because you can then enter a healthier relationship. As you progress, there's more likely to be personal growth, stronger communication and all of the other things that I will discuss in this book that go towards making a high-satisfaction relationship. Those conditions need to be articulated by both partners, ideally towards the beginning of a relationship, but it can also be done retrospectively, to ensure that you are on the same page.

It's about communicating boundaries, mutual respect and strong communication. Ultimately, what you're saying is that you want to feel respected. And in order to feel respected, you need some things to be done and some things not to be done. So, you have to have those discussions. And what inevitably ends up happening, because of the ebb and flow of a relationship, is that you or your partner will do things that neither of you thought about in advance, so negotiation (another form of conflict resolution) will be needed. It's about communicating your conditions up front, and then constantly recalibrating them throughout the course of the relationship.

Love is not an idealised, unconditional state. If you have that philosophy, I believe you will inevitably neglect the everyday interactions and adjustments that need to be made, so make sure you don't miss the weeds that are growing in the garden. The author, psychotherapist and motivational speaker Richard Carlson came up with the phrase 'Don't sweat the small stuff,' which he then used as the title for his bestselling book.[9] I now see people posting and saying it all the time, but in business and especially in relationships you've got to sweat the hell out of the small stuff, because it's the small stuff that's going to get you. Those moments are what add up to create the wound that could cause real danger to your relationship. Most relationships that fail don't do so because of one big thing — they fail because there have been a hundred little things, and it is the hundred and first little thing that pushes the relationship over the edge. If you can set out the conditions that are important to you both, you will be much better placed to deal with the small stuff, thereby giving you the best chance to thrive.

SELF-GUIDED INTERVENTION: VALUING RELATIONSHIP MENTORSHIP AND ESTABLISHING THE CONDITIONS THAT MATTER

OBJECTIVE

To explore the value of relationship mentorship while also guiding you in identifying, setting and recalibrating the conditions that matter most to you and your partner.

INTRODUCTION

Relationship mentorship is a powerful tool that offers guidance and perspective from those who are further ahead in their relationship journey. In addition to learning from mentors, it is equally important to establish and communicate the core conditions that you and your partner need to feel respected, supported and fulfilled. This practice of setting conditions will create clarity in your relationship, reduce misunderstandings and foster personal growth for both you and your partner. This intervention helps ensure mutual respect, clear communication and the creation of a foundation for long-term satisfaction in a relationship.

PART I: FINDING AND UTILISING A RELATIONSHIP MENTOR

1. UNDERSTAND THE CONCEPT OF MENTORSHIP

- A mentor is a couple who have already experienced the challenges that you currently or might one day face. By learning from their journey, you can gain valuable insight into how to navigate relationship dynamics more effectively.
- Mentors can help you understand how they identified the conditions that were important to their relationship and how they negotiated these conditions with their partner.

2. IDENTIFY THE VALUE OF MENTORSHIP IN SETTING CONDITIONS

- Relationship mentors often have valuable advice on how they approached discussing and negotiating relationship conditions. These could include lifestyle preferences, emotional needs, financial priorities or even how they navigated major life decisions.
- Example: A mentor couple may share how they established conditions around managing work–life balance early in their relationship to avoid future conflicts.

3. FIND A MENTOR

- Reach out to couples who are ahead in their relationship journey — whether they're family members, friends or people in your community. These mentors can provide real-life examples of how they worked through their own relationship challenges.
- Example: 'We admire how you've navigated challenges in your relationship. Could we check in with you occasionally to learn from your experience?'

4. USE MENTORSHIP TO REFLECT ON YOUR OWN RELATIONSHIP CONDITIONS

- During your conversations with mentors, ask how they approached the task of establishing conditions in their relationship. Take note of what strategies they used and reflect on how you might apply similar approaches in your own partnership.

- Example: 'How did you both communicate your needs around spending time together versus maintaining individual hobbies?'

PART 2: ESTABLISHING THE CONDITIONS THAT MATTER TO YOU

I. UNDERSTAND THE IMPORTANCE OF CONDITIONS

- Conditions are the fundamental needs and expectations you bring to a relationship. They help ensure that you feel respected, secure and fulfilled. These conditions might relate to emotional support, communication style, personal space, financial goals or even how much social time each partner needs.
- Setting conditions early and revisiting them throughout the relationship leads to stronger personal growth, better communication and higher relationship satisfaction.

2. IDENTIFY YOUR KEY CONDITIONS

- Reflect on what is most important to you in a relationship. What do you need from your partner to feel respected, valued and supported? Consider emotional, physical and lifestyle-related conditions.
- Example: 'It's important for me to have uninterrupted time for my hobbies on weekends, as it helps me recharge for the week ahead.'

3. ARTICULATE YOUR CONDITIONS WITH YOUR PARTNER

- Once you've identified your key conditions, share them openly with your partner. Make sure to explain why these conditions are important to you and how they contribute to your well-being.
- Example: 'I need us to prioritise quality time together at least once a week without distractions. It helps me feel connected to you.'

4. ENGAGE IN A CONDITIONS-SETTING CONVERSATION

- Sit down with your partner in a calm and neutral environment. Each of you should take turns articulating your conditions and explaining why they matter. Actively listen to one another and explore how you can support each other's needs.
- Example: 'Let's both share the things we need to feel happy and supported in this relationship. How can we create a balance that works for both of us?'

5. RECALIBRATE CONDITIONS AS THE RELATIONSHIP GROWS

- As your relationship evolves, so will your needs. Revisit your conditions regularly and be open to adjusting them based on new life stages, circumstances or challenges. Flexibility is key to maintaining a healthy, evolving relationship.
- Example: 'We've started working different shifts lately, and I feel like we haven't had as much time together. Can we find a way to adjust our schedules to make sure we're still connecting?'

PART 3: ESTABLISHING THE CONDITIONS THAT MATTER AS A STAND-ALONE METHOD

I. HOLD A 'CONDITIONS-SETTING MEETING'

- If mentorship is not available, you and your partner can hold a dedicated 'conditions-setting meeting'. This is similar to a state-of-the-union meeting (see page 38), where you both focus on identifying and discussing the key conditions each of you needs to feel respected and supported.
- Example: 'Let's take some time to talk about what's been working well and where we need to adjust our conditions for the future.'

2. SET CLEAR CONDITIONS AROUND SPECIFIC AREAS

- Focus on specific areas of the relationship where conditions might need to be set. These areas could include communication habits, emotional needs, division of responsibilities, financial goals or boundaries around social activities.

- Example: 'I need us to be clear about our financial goals so that we can both feel secure. Let's set a condition where we check in on our budget every month.'

3. REVISIT THE CONVERSATION REGULARLY

- Conditions need to be revisited and adjusted over time. Schedule regular check-ins, similar to state-of-the-union meetings, where both of you can reflect on whether your conditions are being met and if any adjustments need to be made.
- Example: 'It's been a few months since we talked about our personal space needs. Are you still feeling like we have the right balance?'

4. USE THESE MEETINGS TO PREVENT ESCALATING CONFLICTS

- Discussing conditions regularly helps prevent misunderstandings or unmet needs from escalating into larger conflicts. These check-ins create a space for proactive problem-solving rather than reactive conflict resolution.
- Example: 'I noticed that we've been arguing more about housework lately. Let's revisit our conditions around how we divide those responsibilities.'

CONCLUSION

By combining relationship mentorship with the process of setting and revisiting relationship conditions, you can create a framework for long-term success. Mentors offer valuable guidance on navigating challenges, while clear communication around personal conditions helps ensure both you and your partner feel respected, valued and understood.

THE INTERVENTION IN PRACTICE

The first mentors in my and Jill's relationship were a couple I consider to be my uncle and aunt. It was more by accident than design that they became our mentors, thanks to our close proximity to them. The beauty is that they are about five years older than us, so they were always roughly five years ahead of us on their relationship journey, whether it was getting married, moving in together or having their first major blowout. We witnessed all of these things happening, and we were able to talk to them about them. Therefore, when all of those things happened to us, we had perspective and awareness. And particularly when it came to something more challenging, we had confidence that we would be able to deal with it, because my aunt and uncle had always found the answers. It's hands down the best thing that ever happened to our relationship.

Mentorship also comes in different forms. Jill and I were formerly relationship mentors to one couple over WhatsApp. I communicated with one partner and Jill the other. It wasn't therefore about having long conversations — it was more a case of, 'Hey, I was thinking about this. What's your opinion?' Or, 'Do you ever think about this?' We created a bit more structure around it than that, but it was pretty informal, and it didn't require a huge amount of effort on our part, so I'm sure it is the sort of thing many people would be able to replicate if you asked them.

TAKEAWAY

Whether through mentorship or a dedicated conditions-setting process, creating and recalibrating the conditions that matter to you is essential for maintaining a healthy and fulfilling relationship. Clear communication and regular check-ins will help you and your partner grow together, meet each other's needs and navigate the inevitable challenges that arise.

'DELAYED INTERVENTIONS MEAN THAT YOU ULTIMATELY HAVE DEEPER ISSUES TO ADDRESS'

MYTH 4

ONLY COUPLES WHO ARE GOING THROUGH A DIFFICULT TIME GET THERAPY

Provocative Truth: Couples therapy is most effective when undertaken before major problems arise, as it helps strengthen the relationship and prevent future issues

Couples therapy started to take off in the 1950s in the USA and Europe, instigated by people like John Bowlby and Mary Ainsworth, the godfather and godmother of attachment theory.[1*] When it started, it was specifically an intervention for when couples were breaking down and their relationships were at their worst — perhaps there was domestic violence, or the couple, usually spouses, were ready to separate, which was becoming more common around that time. Additionally, at the outset of couples therapy, it was for the most part only for upper-middle-class white people in the Western

---

* Attachment theory has been an area of psychological study since the 1960s. There are four categories of attachment in adults: secure, anxious — preoccupied, dismissive — avoidant and fearful — avoidant. These closely follow the three childhood categories of secure, anxious — ambivalent and avoidant, with the exception that the avoidant category is further differentiated and split in two in adults.

world. The majority of people didn't have access to it, which led to the widespread perception that it was something a bit strange that privileged people did. And, once again, the belief was that it was for couples who were facing severe issues. So, just a short while ago, what has now become a myth was not a myth — it was a fact.

Fast-forward to the 1970s and John Gottman became one of the first psychologists to investigate using couples therapy not just as an intervention once severe issues had developed, but as a preventative measure. This work was taken on by people such as Sue Johnson, who is best known for her development of attachment theory and emotionally focused therapy (EFT) for couples and families. This recognition that couples therapy could be a preventative intervention progressed to the point that some couples even undertook premarital therapy, and subsequent studies have shown that couples who engage in premarital counselling end up having higher satisfaction in their relationships.[2] So, we've reached a point where today you could argue that couples therapy is actually best undertaken when your relationship is not in trouble.

Why, then, does this myth persist? First, there is the cultural aspect. The 1950s were only yesterday in the grand scheme of things. My grandfather came to England from Jamaica in the 1950s, which is just two generations back. So, culturally, couples therapy is still a very new concept. And, as I've just mentioned, it's a concept that was really tucked away for all but the most privileged in the West.

Therapy was initially introduced to the masses through television and the movies. When you watch television now, therapy is still most often mentioned as an option for addressing the most severe issues: these two can't stand each other and fight all the time so they need to see a therapist. As a result, this misconception about what therapy is and what it can be used for is further embedded in society.

Celebrities compound this perception even further. Ben Affleck and Jennifer Garner announced that their marriage was going through issues so they were going through therapy.[3] Will Smith and Jada Pinkett Smith did the same when they were going through a rocky patch.[4] The implication is that we have problems, so we go to therapy. It's easy to then infer that if you don't have issues, you don't go to therapy. And the fact that therapy is not widespread, even to this day, with long waiting lists in the UK, for example, not to mention the cost, means that couples therapy is still not mainstream. As a result, people don't fully understand what therapy is. For example, I strongly believe that therapy is quite simply healing from emotional distress. And it's something that we can do quite a bit on our own, although it's much more effective if you are guided by a professional.

So, there's a misconception about what therapy is. There is a lack of accessibility to therapists. And most people probably don't know very many couples who have seen a therapist, so it's not mainstream. It hasn't entered the ether like online dating has. Online dating was once this weird thing that a very small number of people did, but now the majority of single people have tried it at some point. And, because of all of these factors, stigma still plays a part as well.

However, in most Western countries, there is a more accepting attitude towards therapy today. In Asian countries, such as Japan, South Korea and China, social norms are on average more traditional, with high value assigned to family and privacy, so therapy is not widely accepted in the community. The predominant attitude is that the family should be able to step in and help a couple to resolve their problems. The same goes for Middle Eastern countries, and in most African countries the opinion of therapy is even lower. In Latin America, couples therapy is on the rise, but attitudes towards it are still mixed. So, only in a sliver of the world is therapy even close to being normalised, and where it is more accepted, it's only considered to be a crisis management tool. There's a long way to go.

DON'T LEAVE IT TOO LATE TO GET HELP

There are a number of downsides to this idea of what therapy is and who it is for. Delayed interventions mean that you ultimately have deeper issues to address. By the time you've waited, the problem that was already severe has reached the point where it can actually break up the relationship. For example, there could be growing resentment over the division of labour and household equity, with one person believing that they are doing more of the work than their partner, which is a common problem in relationships. Without a conversation about it, or without any therapy to address it, the issue deepens, and you get to a point where it becomes critical. If you then see a therapist, there are higher stakes, which does a disservice to what therapy can be. If the rowing couple had just come in initially, the therapist would have had a less intense issue to deal with. But now because that one issue around the division of labour has grown and the resentment has escalated, there's more pressure on the therapist. This is also why lower satisfaction rates with therapists are being reported, because more often than not they have to deal with the most severe issues.

Next is that leaving therapy until your problems have worsened increases stress and conflict. You're more likely to have disagreements about the fact that you want to go to the game or do something with your friends. There is more questioning, and one unresolved problem leads to two, which leads to four, which further increases the stress and pressure on the relationship. This can then spill over to affect your friends, family and even community, because whatever problems are happening in your house, your neighbour most likely knows.

Then, lastly, there's a missed opportunity for growth. The only way you are likely to become self-evolved is if you do the work on yourself, and a therapist is best placed to direct you. So, by not having therapy when things are good, not only do you increase the likelihood of stress and conflict, you're also not growing. And that's ultimately what we want to be doing.

I'm a huge advocate for seeing a therapist. That being said, I strongly believe that we can do a lot, if not most, of the work ourselves. And it simply involves partners who want to put effort into strengthening their relationship. That's it, that's all it requires. Now, if you have a partner who is not willing to put in the effort, which will happen from time to time, it's still worth you putting in the effort yourself, because that effort will help you to improve your overall well-being.

IT STARTS WITH AWARENESS

Being aware of and understanding your personal responsibility for making the relationship succeed in order that you both grow as individuals is incredibly important. Similar to active listening, you need to start with an internal awareness about your own responsibilities. Let's say someone has a partner who commits an act of infidelity, and their response is to say, 'My partner is just an asshole. That's the reason why this happened.' Even in those circumstances, yes, their partner probably is an asshole, but there is still value in identifying if there is anywhere in the relationship where they also bear responsibility. To emphasise, I'm not saying that person is to blame for or deserves their partner cheating on them; I'm just saying that it is helpful if they ask themselves if they bear any level of responsibility. For example, perhaps they didn't set out their boundaries early in the relationship. The point is always to understand what part we played in any scenario, because we are only in control of ourselves. We can't control anyone else's behaviour. We can inspire it, but we can't control it, and we can't manage it. So, it starts with us.

Awareness involves educating yourself and your part-ner. That's where it begins. The second step is normalising the conversation. Have lots of small discussions first, perhaps talking about an issue a couple you know is going through. Then you could move on to talking about the intricacies of your own relationship.

Beyond therapy and reading this book, you can do workshops and seminars, together or separately. Frequent check-ins are also effective to gauge how you are both feeling at any given time. How are we doing as a couple right now? How are we feeling together? How strong do we feel? What are the areas where we feel weak? If the effort is there, if the normalisation of the conversation is there and the education is there — and, remember, education never ends — when you have a check-in and realise something is amiss, you're ready to address it. And by doing so, you can heal from emotional distress — such as unspoken resentments, fear of vulnerability, anticipatory anxiety, emotional drift, conflict avoidance, stress management, balancing independence and togetherness, fear of change, sexual intimacy, unrealistic expectations, parenting stress and comparisons to others — or even prevent it from occurring in the first place.

As a result, you have better communication, which is an important aspect of allowing you to self-evolve. Second, you prevent the escalation of minor issues. Third, you deepen your intimacy, because the highest level of emotional intimacy is ultimately what we're striving for. And last, and this could even be the most important, you build resilience as a couple. There's individual resilience and then there's resilience as a couple. Some couples have thin papier mâché walls around their relationship, and if anything hits them, it breaks right through and destroys the relationship, whereas others have Mark Zuckerberg-level bomb-resistant bunkers. That's what you're looking for as a couple, and the best way to achieve it is by taking a proactive approach to therapy, whether that is in a formal context or you and your partner choosing to work on your relationship yourselves.

SELF-GUIDED INTERVENTION: USING PROACTIVE THERAPY EARLY IN A RELATIONSHIP TO STRENGTHEN BONDS

OBJECTIVE

To introduce the concept of proactive therapy and open, continuous communication early in your relationship as a means of strengthening bonds, preventing conflicts and building resilience.

INTRODUCTION

A healthy relationship takes work, and awareness of that is the first step. This intervention will show you that proactive therapy, along with open communication and continuous education, isn't just a last resort but a tool for growth, intimacy and long-term success. The steps will help you and your partner build stronger emotional connections, navigate challenges before they escalate and deepen intimacy. By normalising discussions around sensitive topics early on, you can prevent minor issues from snowballing into larger conflicts.

PART I: AWARENESS AND RESPONSIBILITY IN THE RELATIONSHIP

I. DEVELOP AWARENESS OF YOURSELF AND YOUR ROLE IN THE RELATIONSHIP

- Recognise a healthy relationship requires effort and self-awareness. Understand your personal responsibility in contributing to the relationship's success and growth.
- Example: Even in challenging situations (like a partner's mistake), consider where you might bear some responsibility for the health of the relationship and for managing conflict styles. This doesn't mean blaming yourself for your partner's actions but focusing on what you can control: your own behaviour and expectations.

2. ENGAGE IN FREQUENT 'CHECK-INS'

- Regular check-ins with your partner can be informal but should focus on general feelings and the state of your relationship. Unlike state-of-the-union meetings that focus on a single topic, check-ins are about gauging your emotional and relational health as a couple.
- Example: 'How are we doing as a couple right now? Is there anything we should work on or improve?'

PART 2: PROACTIVE THERAPY AND CONTINUOUS EDUCATION

I. UNDERSTAND THAT THERAPY ISN'T A LAST RESORT

- Attending therapy, workshops or relationship seminars early in a relationship is a proactive way to build communication skills and resilience. By engaging in therapy early on, couples can address underlying issues before they become serious problems.
- Example: Consider scheduling therapy sessions as a form of relationship maintenance, even if nothing feels 'wrong'. Therapy can help facilitate conversations and provide tools for navigating conflicts.

2. EDUCATE YOURSELF AND YOUR PARTNER

- A relationship thrives on continued learning. Educating yourself and your partner about relationship dynamics, emotional health and conflict resolution can improve your ability to navigate challenges together.
- Example: Read relationship books, listen to podcasts or attend workshops together. Normalise learning about relationships as part of the process, not just as something you do when there's a problem.

3. NORMALISE SENSITIVE CONVERSATIONS

- Start by acknowledging that any relationship will face difficulties and that talking about sensitive subjects can prevent issues from escalating. Normalising discussions around emotions, needs and even difficult topics early in a relationship helps build openness and trust.

- Example: Watch a relationship show like *Married at First Sight* together, then ask your partner their thoughts on a situation: 'Do you agree with what Paul said? Why?' That way, you are addressing a more difficult topic, but it's not about you; it's about these people you've never met on TV.

- Graduate towards more personal, intimate topics. As you build this practice, you'll reduce stigma and break down barriers to discussing difficult subjects.

- Example: After discussing a TV couple's situation, talk about how a mutual friend handled a relationship challenge. Then, over time, bring these discussions closer to home, sharing your own feelings or needs more openly.

PART 3: THE BENEFITS OF PROACTIVE THERAPY AND OPEN COMMUNICATION

I. PREVENT ESCALATION OF MINOR ISSUES

- Proactive therapy and frequent check-ins help address small issues before they become bigger. By maintaining an open dialogue, you can prevent misunderstandings from building up and turning into conflicts.

- Example: A minor annoyance, such as feeling ignored during a busy period, can be addressed early on before it grows into resentment or distance.

2. BUILD EMOTIONAL INTIMACY AND RESILIENCE

- Emotional intimacy grows when both partners feel heard, respected and valued. Proactive conversations and therapy sessions deepen the connection by creating a safe space to express vulnerabilities.

- Example: Couples who continuously engage in open discussions are more likely to feel emotionally connected, making them more resilient during tough times.

3. STRENGTHEN THE RELATIONSHIP'S RESILIENCE

- Relationships that engage in proactive therapy and constant communication build a form of resilience, akin to creating 'strong walls' around the relationship. You're better equipped to handle life's challenges without the relationship breaking down.
- Example: Regular therapy sessions and check-ins are like 'reinforcements' that strengthen your relationship against external pressures.

4. FOCUS ON MUTUAL GROWTH

- Proactive therapy encourages individual and relational growth. As you each learn more about yourselves and your partnership, you can grow together, fostering personal development and shared goals.
- Example: Therapy isn't just about fixing problems — it's about fostering personal responsibility, self-awareness and mutual growth.

PART 4: MAKING PROACTIVE THERAPY A REGULAR PART OF YOUR RELATIONSHIP

I. MAKE THERAPY AND CHECK-INS PART OF YOUR ROUTINE

- Consider scheduling regular check-ins or therapy sessions as part of your relationship routine. This could be monthly or quarterly sessions, even if everything is going well.
- Example: 'Let's set a time each month to talk about how we're doing. Even if we feel good now, it's important to stay on the same page.'

2. BE OPEN AND HONEST IN THERAPY

- Therapy works best when both partners are open and willing to address even the smallest of issues. Practise being vulnerable and sharing your thoughts honestly during sessions.
- Example: 'I've been feeling a bit distant lately because of work stress, and I wanted to talk about how we can stay connected even when we're busy.'

3. USE THERAPY AS A TOOL FOR LONG-TERM SUCCESS

- Therapy isn't just a tool for crisis management — it's a tool for long-term relationship success. Over time, therapy and continuous communication help create a relationship that is strong, emotionally intimate and built on mutual understanding.
- Example: Couples who engage in proactive therapy tend to navigate future conflicts with more ease and confidence, knowing they have the tools and communication skills to handle them.

CONCLUSION

Proactive therapy, combined with regular check-ins and open communication, is a powerful way to strengthen your relationship from the beginning. Therapy is not a last resort — it's a proactive approach to building resilience, intimacy and trust. By engaging in these practices early on, you and your partner can foster mutual growth, prevent conflict escalation and ensure that your relationship is built on a solid foundation.

THE INTERVENTION IN PRACTICE

An aspect of my relationship with Jill that I really enjoy is that, because of the work we do, we have normalised having a conversation about almost anything. So, for example, I read *Mind the Gap* by Dr Karen Gurney in preparation for a podcast I was doing with her, and in it she talks about the orgasm gap, which is a reference to the fact that women typically report that the number and strength of their orgasms decline over time. I mentioned this to Jill, and she said it was happening to her. I hadn't realised, so it was such an important conversation to have, and we were able to have it in the first place because we've normalised having conversations around these sensitive subjects. By doing so, you reduce stigma, myths and misconceptions.

TAKEAWAY

A relationship requires continuous work and commitment. Proactive therapy, education and open communication provide the tools needed to build a relationship that thrives on emotional intimacy, resilience and personal growth. Start therapy early and normalise conversations about your needs and feelings to ensure long-term success in your partnership.

'A HEALTHY DOUBT IS
ONE THAT ARISES FROM
A QUESTION AROUND
MUTUAL GROWTH'

MYTH 5

HAVING DOUBTS ABOUT YOUR RELATIONSHIP IS A RED FLAG

Provocative Truth: Having doubts in a relationship is normal and can foster deeper trust and connection

Overall, I think there's this notion that we need to be certain about who our partner is, what their intentions are and what our compatibility is at all times. And if we are not certain, if we have any doubt, then it's indicative of a weak or bad relationship. And I think what you often see happening with a lot of couples early on is that the moment one or both of them begins to have any doubts, which are actually healthy doubts, they interpret that as their partner not being right for them and they break up.

THE DIFFERENCE BETWEEN HEALTHY AND UNHEALTHY DOUBTS

To my mind, a healthy doubt is one that arises from a question around mutual growth. Are you compatible in the long term? Is your partner giving you enough? Are you growing in the relationship? Is there balance, equity and equality in the partnership? These are healthy doubts. Another example of a legitimate doubt that you might not want to vocalise because you don't want to be disruptive is not liking your partner's best friend. But for the purposes of mutual growth, I think it's a healthy doubt to expose. It's the sort of thing that could potentially fester and get worse if it is not expressed. Unhealthy doubts, on the other hand, are driven by insecurities and past trauma, and don't necessarily speak to mutual growth. So, it could be jealousy. It could be having continual distrust of your partner. It could be catastrophising the relationship.

The point of this chapter, therefore, is to challenge the myth that you shouldn't have any doubts, and instead acknowledge that some doubts are healthy doubts and can actually strengthen your relationship.

As with many cultural norms, the need for certainty partly seems to stem from the Middle Ages. In the Arthurian legends, the moment Lancelot and Guinevere see one another, they are sure that they are the perfect match. And even though their coming together creates all types of problems, it doesn't matter to them, because they believe that they're the perfect fit. This idea of love at first sight has, over the years, become ingrained in Western society in particular. From romcoms to romantic novels, there are countless examples of narratives that support this myth. Perhaps one of the best examples of this is Noah and Allie from *The Notebook* — even through long separations and life's many challenges, they never waver in their belief that they are meant to be together. You see this myth in other areas of pop culture too. The cornerstone of the celebrity couple is often built on the same idea of destined love. It's why we rooted for Ben Affleck and Jennifer Lopez when they found their way back to each other, despite the ups and downs, and why we felt the heartbreak of Brad Pitt and Angelina Jolie's break-up. While any skilled therapist would offer a more nuanced view of relationships, as we explored in the previous chapter, couples therapy is still not widespread or normalised. As a result, these idealised narratives often persist unchallenged in popular culture.

The consequences of believing absolute certainty is the bedrock of a successful relationship can be really serious. For example, it can lead to the suppression of emotions, which has a negative effect on your well-being. In a paper by psychologists James Gross and Oliver John, they show that the suppression of doubt can lead to several negative outcomes.[1] One is increased stress, because you're spending cognitive power to keep the feelings of doubt at bay, which will have a knock-on effect on your physical well-being — for example, it has been shown that prolonged periods of stress can weaken your immune system. The suppression of feelings can also lead to difficulty in the processing of emotions, because you're not familiar with how to deal with them through practice and experience. Ultimately, it lowers your satisfaction in the relationship and weakens intimacy, particularly if you believe that you are the cause of the uncertainty, which, in turn, lowers your overall sense of subjective well-being. So, a chain reaction happens when you suppress your feelings.

Another problem with believing that you should never have doubts in your relationship is that it can lead to unrealistic expectations. If you think that your relationship should be perfect, the moment there are any doubts you inevitably feel a disproportionate level of disappointment that you have not been able to keep them at bay.

Rejecting doubt can also lead to you searching for perfection. But becoming self-actualised and having high satisfaction does not mean being in a perfect relationship. If you're saying that you're looking for more from your relationship than you ever have before, and you want to achieve self-actualisation, it could seem like perfection is the ultimate goal, but that's not what we're talking about. To me, the best way to think about this is the notion of destination versus the process. Self-actualisation is actually the process — it's not the destination. If perfection is the destination, you'll never get there. It's another example of unrealistic expectations.

You can also end up making impulsive decisions as a result of trying to avoid or deny doubt. Like hurrying into marriage to avoid addressing any critical issues. Or rushing to move because your partner wants to. Whatever it may be, impulsive decisions equal poor relationship outcomes.[2]

There's also a tipping point to all of this, and some doubts are genuine signs of things that are wrong or need to be addressed. Sometimes uncertainty or doubt might actually be telling you something. So, it's not about ignoring all doubts, or trying to focus only on positive doubts — there will be situations where there is a deeper problem. That's why it's so important that you voice your doubts, as opposed to what a lot of people do in this situation, which is to not say anything. If you're not discussing how you feel, it will grow into something larger.

THE BENEFIT OF DOUBT

In a paper by John Gottman and Robert Levenson, they explain that, in essence, the more conflict we have, the better we are able to build the skills to resolve that conflict, and building the skills to resolve conflict is what makes us stronger.[3] Within the context of this chapter, doubt is a form of conflict. Doubt challenges the stability and security of a relationship, creating internal tension that, when addressed, provides an opportunity for growth. Just like external disagreements, the internal conflict of doubt forces partners to communicate, seek clarity and reaffirm their commitment. By working through doubt rather than avoiding it, couples develop resilience and a deeper understanding of one another. Ignoring or suppressing doubt, on the other hand, can lead to unresolved issues that undermine trust and intimacy over time.

Thus, doubt, when engaged with productively, can serve as a powerful force for strengthening a relationship.

In another study, this time on emotional honesty and its association with relationship satisfaction, couples who were more open about their feelings, including their uncertainties and insecurities, were found to have higher levels of satisfaction and more stability in their relationships.[4] Honesty, even about doubts, leads to better relationship satisfaction.

And another paper showed that couples who proactively go out of their way to discuss doubts and stresses are able to develop effective coping strategies, which then enhance the resilience of their relationships.[5] And because they have more resilience, when they come across a more challenging hurdle, they'll already have built up the skills to overcome it.

If you embrace and vocalise your doubts, you get enhanced communication, a stronger bond and increased resilience as a result. And, ultimately, what all of those mean together is stronger emotional intimacy. That's really what you should be seeking if self-actualisation is your goal.

HOW TO EXPRESS DOUBT

How you express doubt is also important, and there are many elements that go into how a partner receives a message: context, their well-being, their self-esteem, past insecurities, traumas and so on. I think it's about voicing the doubt when it comes up. That's the key. And it's about working towards having a partnership where you can have a free flow of dialogue.

It's also about getting into the practice of expressing doubt and uncertainty from the outset of your relationship and not waiting until the honeymoon period is over. It makes no sense to wait a year or two before all of a sudden presenting your partner with a doubt or uncertainty that they are completely not expecting, such as questioning whether you both want the same things for your future. It needs to be built into the relationship from the beginning. If you wait, your doubt is likely to be exponentially larger, and the suppression of your feelings could be detrimental to your well-being and the success of your relationship.

This again speaks to expectations. If you go into your relationship thinking that it's got to be perfect, then you're setting yourself up to fail. Social media doesn't help in this regard, with so many accounts posting about what is, at the end of the day, a made-up representation of their lives and relationships. What is needed is a little bit more authenticity about what it really takes to make a relationship work. And we are thankfully seeing more influencers and celebrities who want to expose something that's challenging to them. More of this would help to normalise the doubts that are inevitable in every relationship at some point. The more realistic expectations of Gen Z are also helping us to move in this direction. At Tinder, we see that Gen Zers are more authentically approaching their relationships and have a larger desire to be with someone who they feel they can be their full self with, including any doubts or insecurities, and they use that criterion early in their relationships.

♥

It's completely understandable why you might think that certainty is an integral part of a successful relationship. After all, being in a successful, loving relationship is such an important part of our lives, and it would therefore seem sensible that we would want to get it right and be 100 per cent sure about it at all times. However, nothing in life is perfect, including our relationships, so embracing doubt in a proactive and healthy way can allow you and your partner to flourish.

SELF-GUIDED INTERVENTION: EMBRACING DOUBTS IN A RELATIONSHIP TO FOSTER DEEPER TRUST AND CONNECTION

OBJECTIVE

To normalise having doubts in a relationship and use them as a way to build trust, resilience and deeper emotional intimacy. By understanding that doubts are natural, you can use them to foster open communication, trust and connection, rather than allowing them to fester and escalate into larger issues.

INTRODUCTION

Doubts are a normal part of any relationship and should not be seen as a sign of weakness or failure. In fact, when approached openly, doubts can create opportunities for deeper connection and trust between partners. This intervention will guide you in expressing and addressing doubts, while also focusing on the things you appreciate about your partner to maintain a healthy, balanced perspective.

PART I: ACKNOWLEDGING AND NORMALISING DOUBTS

I. UNDERSTAND THAT DOUBTS ARE NORMAL

- Every relationship experiences periods of doubt. This might be doubt about compatibility, future goals or even whether the relationship is going in the right direction. Recognise that these feelings are a natural part of the relationship cycle and can be used to strengthen, rather than harm, your connection.
- Example: 'It's normal for me to wonder if we're on the same page about our future. Instead of seeing this as a problem, I'll use it as a prompt for an open conversation.'

2. EMBRACE CHECK-INS TO EXPRESS DOUBTS

- Regular check-ins provide a structured opportunity to express doubts before they escalate. By discussing feelings early on, both you and your partner can address concerns in a safe and supportive environment. Research shows that check-ins foster better communication and prevent minor doubts from becoming larger conflicts.

- Example: During a check-in, ask, 'Is there anything that's been on your mind lately that we haven't discussed? How are you feeling about where we are?'

3. USE SHARED ACTIVITIES TO PRACTISE EXPRESSING DOUBT

- Engaging in new or shared activities (such as trying a new sport, cooking together or learning a new skill) offers low-stakes opportunities to express minor doubts. These smaller doubts allow you to practise expressing yourself in ways that will be helpful when addressing more serious concerns in the relationship.
- Example: During a shared activity, you might say, 'I'm not sure if this approach is working for me. What do you think we could do differently?' This kind of language teaches you how to gently express doubts in other areas of the relationship.

PART 2: BUILDING TRUST THROUGH APPRECIATION AND GRATITUDE

I. EXPRESS GRATITUDE REGULARLY

- Regularly expressing what you appreciate about your partner creates a foundation of trust and emotional safety. When your partner feels valued, they're more likely to be open and receptive when doubts or concerns arise.
- Example: 'I really appreciate how supportive you've been of my work projects lately. It means a lot to me to know you're there when I need you.'

2. FOCUS ON WHAT'S GOOD WHILE ACKNOWLEDGING DOUBTS

- While doubts are natural, it's important not to let them overshadow the positive aspects of the relationship. Focus on the qualities that you love about your partner and the things that are working well in your relationship. This balanced perspective makes it easier to address doubts without them becoming overwhelming.
- Example: 'I sometimes worry about how we're handling our long-distance situation, but I know how much we care about each other, and that's the most important thing.'

3. USE GRATITUDE TO SOFTEN THE DISCUSSION OF DOUBTS

- When expressing doubts, start with what you appreciate about your partner to create a positive, open atmosphere. This approach makes it easier for your partner to listen and respond without feeling defensive.
- Example: 'I love how thoughtful you are, and I feel really close to you most of the time. Lately, though, I've had some doubts about how we communicate when we're stressed. Could we talk about that?'

PART 3: ADDRESSING DOUBTS IN A CONSTRUCTIVE WAY

I. ACKNOWLEDGE YOUR DOUBTS OPENLY

- When doubts arise, express them openly, rather than letting them build up. By sharing your feelings early, you create space for dialogue and mutual understanding. Use 'I' statements (see page 34) to keep the conversation focused on your feelings, rather than blaming your partner.
- Example: 'I've been feeling a little uncertain about how we're handling our future plans. I'd love to talk through it with you.'

2. BE HONEST, BUT GENTLE

- Express your doubts honestly, but be gentle in how you frame them. The goal is to open up a conversation, not to criticise or create significant conflict. Speak from a place of curiosity and a desire to understand, rather than frustration or accusation.
- Example: 'I've noticed that we've been avoiding talking about certain things lately, and I'm starting to feel unsure about where we stand. Can we talk about that?'

3. REAFFIRM YOUR COMMITMENT TO THE RELATIONSHIP

- After expressing doubts, reaffirm your commitment to the relationship. This helps your partner feel secure and reinforces that you're sharing your feelings to strengthen the relationship, not to damage it.
- Example: 'Even though I've had these doubts, I'm committed to working through them with you because I believe in us.'

4. USE CHECK-INS FOR CONTINUOUS REFLECTION

- Regular check-ins allow you to revisit any doubts that may have been discussed earlier and ensure that both you and your partner are still feeling good about the direction of the relationship. These check-ins foster trust and help keep doubts from growing into bigger issues.
- Example: 'Last time we talked about feeling disconnected during the week. How do you feel things have been since then? Is there anything else we should work on?'

PART 4: STRENGTHENING THE RELATIONSHIP BY BUILDING RESILIENCE

I. BUILD RESILIENCE THROUGH REGULAR CONVERSATIONS

- Regularly expressing doubts and addressing them constructively builds resilience in your relationship. When both of you feel comfortable discussing uncertainties, the relationship becomes stronger and better equipped to handle challenges in the future.

- Example: 'I'm glad we've been able to talk about our concerns so openly. I feel like it's made us more resilient as a couple.'

2. STRENGTHEN EMOTIONAL INTIMACY THROUGH OPENNESS

- Addressing doubts doesn't weaken a relationship — it deepens emotional intimacy. When both of you feel safe sharing your vulnerabilities, you create a deeper bond that allows you to grow together.
- Example: 'Talking through our doubts has made me feel more connected to you. I'm glad we've been able to work through things together.'

3. FOCUS ON GROWTH AND IMPROVEMENT

- Use the discussions around doubts as opportunities for growth, both individually and as a couple. By tackling doubts head-on, you create space for positive changes and personal growth within the relationship.
- Example: 'I've learned so much about myself through these conversations, and I feel like we've both grown stronger because of them.'

CONCLUSION

Doubts in a relationship are natural and can be an opportunity to build deeper trust, emotional intimacy and resilience. By addressing doubts openly, focusing on what you appreciate about your partner and using regular check-ins and shared activities, you can foster a stronger, healthier relationship.

TAKEAWAY

Embrace doubts as a normal part of the relationship journey and use them as opportunities for growth and deeper connection. Regularly expressing appreciation, engaging in open conversations and addressing concerns early on will help you and your partner build trust, intimacy and long-term resilience.

'QUALITY IS MORE IMPORTANT THAN QUANTITY, AND IT IS ACTUALLY EMOTIONAL CONNECTION RATHER THAN SEXUAL FREQUENCY THAT LEADS TO BETTER SEXUAL SATISFACTION'

MYTH 6

MORE SEX EQUALS A HAPPIER RELATIONSHIP

Provocative Truth: It's the emotional connection, not the frequency of sex, that makes intimacy truly satisfying

I think it's fair to say that many of us believe that the more sex we're having, the happier we are. And, in fact, there is some empirical evidence to back this up. A 2016 study found that sexual frequency does correlate with happiness; however, the effect plateaus at a frequency of once a week.[1] Clinical psychologist and sex expert Dr Karen Gurney, meanwhile, told me that couples have sex three to four times per month on average, which is roughly in line with the figure of once a week being enough to ensure that most people are sexually satisfied, rather than the multiple times a week that I think many people would imagine. So, anything over once a week doesn't mean you're any happier. I think this underscores the fact that high frequency does not equal romantic success.

So where does this idea that you need to be having a lot of sex to be happy come from? Well, the media plays a huge part. From TV dramas and romantic films to dating shows, social media and advertising campaigns, sexual activity is constantly being linked with happiness. Just think about a show such as *Sex and the City*, for example. The characters are only happy when they're having lots of sex, and they're miserable when they're not. It's the same on *Married at First Sight* — the couples all question their relationships if they are not having prolific sex right from the off. And while I don't necessarily think that sex is the most important factor in whether the couples are compatible, I do think the show accurately reflects what often happens in real life. When it is early in the relationship, the couples tend to have a lot of sex. Many of them come and sit on the couch a few weeks after their honeymoons and tell us that they love one another. Because they are having sex like rabbits, they make the leap to thinking that they are in love.

Although she couldn't quantify it when we spoke, Dr Gurney also told me that our grandparents were having significantly more sex than we do, though they did not necessarily equate sex with love to the same degree. The reason for this is that they didn't have the same distractions that we do today: streaming services, social media, the internet, gaming — the list goes on and on. We all have to be busy all of the time. Our grandparents and great-grandparents, on the other hand, didn't have those distractions.

As we've seen, people weren't necessarily focused on self-actualisation or expecting a partner to meet all of their needs in the past. You might have been looking for someone to co-parent, manage the household and share a sexual connection with. Because they sought less overall emotional connection, they were more willing to enjoy specific aspects of the relationship, like sex. Today, however, we expect so much more from our partners. If they fall short in one area (like co-parenting), we're less inclined to engage in other areas (like sex). Instead of finding joy in individual aspects of the relationship, we now expect fulfilment in all areas before we can enjoy any part, including physical intimacy.

With such high expectations on people, it is perhaps no wonder that many people then worry that they're not fulfilling their partner's needs. And if they don't fulfil their partner's needs and have sex as much as they think their partner wants, they think they're going to lose them or their partner's going to cheat on them.

I think the same issues apply to single-sex and non-heteronormative relationships. The average benchmarks may be different in some of those relationships, but ultimately the same myth is perpetuated, which is that if you're not having sex all the time, then you're not satisfied. There was a same-sex couple on a series of *Married at First Sight* who told us one week that they were in love with one another and having lots of sex. The next week when we asked them how they were, they replied they were having a terrible time and not even having sex any more. They were using how often they had sex to assess the quality of their relationship. If they weren't having sex, it was indicative to them that they were in a bad place. Whereas there are many couples who are not having sex but have great emotional intimacy and therefore have strong satisfaction in their relationships.

Of course, I'm not saying you can't have lots of sex within your relationship – you can get a lot of enjoyment out of that – but if you're looking for sex to be the barometer of the health of your relationship, or to give you the emotional intimacy that is necessary to really take your relationship to the next level, you're going to fall short and be disappointed. I'm not here to say that people shouldn't have lots of sex if that's what they want to do. It's just that you have to be realistic about what you're going to get out of that.

The same-sex couple on *Married at First Sight* were focusing on the wrong thing, but there was an element of truth in what they were saying – going from a place of high frequency to no sex at all pointed to the fact that there was some other issue in the relationship. But the lack of sex was the symptom not the cause.

EMOTIONAL INTIMACY IS THE KEY

The outcome of all of the messages around sex, and the way sex is used to sell products and is associated with happiness, is that it's created this misconception that sexual intimacy is correlated with emotional intimacy; whereas, in actual fact, it's only one factor of emotional intimacy, and it is not the be-all and end-all. That's why the plateau when it comes to well-being is having sex on average once a week — sexual desire can be linked to sexual frequency, but sexual desire is just one facet of sexual satisfaction. Sex fulfils one element of emotional intimacy, but it's not everything. Ultimately, it is emotional intimacy that has a direct correlation with our satisfaction in the relationship.

The downsides of believing that sexual intimacy is the same as emotional intimacy can lead to pressure and disappointment. The idea is that because you're not having sex once a day, you're a failure and your relationship is a failure. One study showed that high sexual frequency expectations actually lead to sexual dissatisfaction, due to pressure and anxiety, discrepancy in desire, focus on quantity over quality and a mismatch with reality.[2] Another downside is the neglect of other important aspects of your relationship. If you focus solely on how often you have sex as the area to work on, you might overlook truly undervalued aspects of your relationship that could lead to greater emotional intimacy. For example, you might neglect spending quality time together, such as engaging in shared hobbies or experiences that bring you closer. Similarly, you might overlook the importance of effective communication, such as having open conversations about your feelings, dreams and goals. Both of these are foundational for building a deeper emotional connection and can have a much greater impact on the overall health and intimacy of your relationship than simply focusing on physical intimacy. Concentrating on sexual frequency, on the other hand, can lead to reduced sexual satisfaction overall, because you think you should be doing it. And if you feel like you're having sex for the sake of it and not because you really want to, you will have lower satisfaction.

NURTURING EMOTIONAL INTIMACY

Quality is more important than quantity, and it is actually emotional connection rather than sexual frequency that leads to better sexual satisfaction, which, in turn, leads to better overall relationship satisfaction. One important element of emotional intimacy is feeling safe, and not feeling fearful or threatened by your partner or the environment. That's the first piece of the equation: creating situations and scenarios where you feel completely at ease and where there are no inhibitions or limitations. Dr Gurney told me that the best determination of whether someone is having great sex is that they feel they lose themselves in the moment, and you can't lose yourself in the moment if you don't feel safe.

Preparing yourself to have the best sex in the world does not require taking aphrodisiacs or popping pills. The goal is to be in the moment and stay in the moment without distraction. But many people can't be in the moment just with themselves, let alone with their partners. That's why meditation, yoga and breathing exercises, for example, can all be beneficial for your sex life, as they teach you how to stay present. And this is an extension of emotional intimacy, because you have to be safe and able to be in the moment to have a close connection with a partner. That's a full act of vulnerability, which is indicative of emotional intimacy.

Something that comes up a lot when I talk to women about sex is their fear of showing their bodies to their partners and wanting to make sure that they have clothes on or that the lights are off when they have sex. I completely get it — many of us feel self-conscious about our bodies from time to time. However, if you are in a committed relationship and still feel this way, it could suggest that you don't feel entirely safe in your partnership. If, on the other hand, you are able to work on your emotional intimacy and create an environment of complete trust, physical intimacy becomes a lot easier.

Especially in same-sex relationships, there is a common misconception that orgasm is the ultimate objective of sex and that full satisfaction can only be achieved through penetration, particularly for men. But Dr Gurney, along with renowned sex researchers such as Masters and Johnson, would argue that sexual satisfaction is deeply personal and can be defined in many ways. Emotional and physical intimacy don't require penetration or orgasm to be fulfilling. Instead, the true essence of satisfaction comes from losing yourself in the moment, in whatever form that takes, and sharing that experience with a partner. This process fosters strong emotional intimacy, which ultimately leads to greater sexual satisfaction. However, to break away from traditional expectations or 'scripts' around sex, there must be a foundation of emotional intimacy with your partner. Therefore, we need to rethink and broaden our understanding of what qualifies as satisfying sex, focusing less on specific acts and more on the quality of the emotional connection.

The reason emotional connection can enhance sexual satisfaction and provide higher levels of satisfaction and well-being is again connected to safety and fear. If you have the highest level of emotional intimacy, you are able to explore limitlessly, communicate your desires and lose yourself in the moment. Dr Gurney says that she can correlate sexual satisfaction with the strength of communication in a relationship. If the communication is poor, everything else is most likely going to be poor too, including the sex. And if that is the case, it is possible to have a high frequency of sex but low satisfaction. Like a lot of the things we're talking about in this book, being able to communicate your emotional needs, this time around sex, is a good skill to have in general, as it speaks to your ability to communicate about any other potentially difficult topic that might come up.

SELF-GUIDED INTERVENTION: PRIORITISING EMOTIONAL INTIMACY OVER QUANTITY OF SEX TO STRENGTHEN YOUR RELATIONSHIP

OBJECTIVE

To strengthen emotional intimacy and connection in your relationship, leading to a more fulfilling and satisfying sexual relationship.

INTRODUCTION

Many people believe that the frequency of sex is what strengthens relationships, but research and experience show that it's the quality of your emotional connection that truly fuels lasting intimacy. This intervention focuses on the quality of your emotional bond rather than the quantity of sexual activity, demonstrating how emotional closeness enhances sexual desire and connection. The steps will help you focus on strengthening emotional intimacy through mindfulness, communication and scheduled quality time, which can lead to a more satisfying sex life.

PART I: BUILDING EMOTIONAL INTIMACY THROUGH PRESENCE AND MINDFULNESS

I. PRACTISE MINDFULNESS WITH YOUR PARTNER

- Emotional intimacy starts with being fully present with your partner. Practising mindfulness together, even in small ways, can strengthen your connection.
- Set a 'no phubbing' rule during shared activities. Whether you're at dinner or on a walk, make a conscious effort to put your phone aside and focus on being present with one another.

- Example: 'During our next meal, let's put our phones away and really focus on enjoying one another's company.'

2. ENGAGE IN NON-SEXUAL TOUCH

- Physical intimacy doesn't always have to be sexual. The Masters and Johnson method, known as sensate focus, encourages couples to engage in non-sexual touch, such as holding hands, hugging or touching each other's arms.[3] This helps make physical intimacy feel more natural and familiar, which can lead to more comfort and connection during sexual moments.
- Example: Spend five minutes every day sitting close to each other, simply touching in a non-sexual way — whether holding hands, rubbing each other's backs or resting your head on your partner's shoulder.

3. SCHEDULE INTIMACY SESSIONS TO COMMUNICATE OPENLY

- Scheduled intimacy sessions where you talk about sexual desires, doubts and needs — without necessarily engaging in sexual activity — create a safe space for communication. These conversations strengthen emotional intimacy, leading to better understanding and satisfaction in the relationship.
- Example: Set aside time once a week to sit down and talk about how you're both feeling in terms of intimacy. Use this time to express any concerns or desires, and to check in on each other's emotional well-being.

PART 2: PRIORITISING EMOTIONAL INTIMACY OVER SPONTANEITY

I. FOCUS ON THE QUALITY OF EMOTIONAL INTIMACY

- Emotional intimacy is the foundation for a satisfying sexual relationship. When you focus on emotional closeness, sexual desire naturally follows. Even if sex is less frequent, the connection will be more meaningful and satisfying.

- Example: Spend time each day talking about your feelings, your day and your emotional needs. These daily conversations help build closeness and trust, which are key to strong intimacy.

2. SCHEDULE TIME FOR INTIMACY WITHOUT THE PRESSURE OF SEX

- While spontaneity may seem romantic to some people (see Chapter 18 for more on this), scheduling time for intimacy can be just as effective. Scheduling creates the space for connection in the midst of busy lives, allowing you to be fully present with each other when the moment arrives.
- Example: Schedule a weekly 'intimacy night' where you spend time together, whether or not it leads to sex. The goal is to relax, connect emotionally and enjoy each other's company.

3. USE ANTICIPATION TO BUILD DESIRE

- Anticipation can be a powerful tool in enhancing desire. Sending flirty texts during the day, recalling a romantic or intimate moment or sharing what you're looking forward to that evening can build excitement.
- Example: Send a text while your partner is at work, saying, 'I've been thinking about that night when we stayed up talking and cuddling. Let's recreate it tonight.'

PART 3: STRENGTHENING EMOTIONAL INTIMACY LEADS TO BETTER SEXUAL DESIRE

I. ACKNOWLEDGE THAT DESIRE FOLLOWS EMOTIONAL CONNECTION

- Sexual desire is often the result of emotional closeness. By focusing on building emotional intimacy, you naturally create an environment where sexual desire can flourish.

- Example: After a day of emotionally connecting with your partner, you may notice that your desire to be physically intimate is stronger because of the emotional groundwork you've laid.

2. UNDERSTAND THAT SPONTANEITY IS A BY-PRODUCT, NOT A REQUIREMENT

- While spontaneous sex may seem ideal, it's not necessary for a fulfilling relationship. Strong emotional intimacy can lead to moments of spontaneity, but don't pressure yourself or your partner to be spontaneous all the time. The key is feeling connected and comfortable, which is what truly fosters desire. We'll discuss this in more detail in Chapter 18.
- Example: Plan to spend time together without putting pressure on spontaneous sex. The emotional connection built during those moments may naturally lead to intimacy when the timing feels right.

3. BUILD RESILIENCE THROUGH EMOTIONAL INTIMACY

- Couples who focus on building emotional intimacy are better equipped to handle life's pressures while still maintaining closeness and connection.
- Example: When life gets busy, check in with each other emotionally. Make time to talk about what's going on in your lives and support each other through challenges. This emotional support will deepen your bond and keep your intimacy strong.

PART 4: PRACTISING GRATITUDE AND APPRECIATION FOR YOUR PARTNER

I. REGULARLY EXPRESS WHAT YOU APPRECIATE

- Expressing appreciation for your partner's qualities and the things they do for you helps strengthen your emotional connection. This positive reinforcement builds trust and affection, laying the groundwork for a more fulfilling intimate relationship.

- Example: 'I really appreciate how supportive you've been during this busy week. It makes me feel so loved.'

2. COMBINE GRATITUDE WITH INTIMACY

- Before you begin any intimate moment, express something you're grateful for about your partner. This enhances emotional closeness and sets the stage for more connected and meaningful physical intimacy.
- Example: Before an intimate night, say, 'I love how safe and supported you make me feel, and I'm so grateful for our connection.'

3. BUILD TRUST THROUGH VULNERABILITY

- When you open up emotionally, you build trust with your partner. This trust creates a space where both of you feel safe exploring your desires and intimacy without fear of judgement or rejection.
- Example: During your intimacy sessions, share something you've been feeling vulnerable about. This openness can deepen your connection and lead to more fulfilling intimacy.

CONCLUSION

Focusing on the quality of your emotional connection, rather than the quantity of sex, strengthens the bond between you and your partner. Emotional intimacy lays the foundation for a more satisfying sexual relationship by building trust, comfort and desire. Through mindfulness, regular communication and shared appreciation, you can deepen your emotional connection with your partner and create a fulfilling, long-lasting partnership.

TAKEAWAY

Emotional intimacy is the cornerstone of a strong and satisfying relationship. By prioritising connection, practising mindfulness and regularly expressing gratitude, you can strengthen your bond and create an environment where sexual desire and satisfaction naturally flourish.

'TAKING A PAUSE IS NOT
ENOUGH ON ITS OWN –
IT IS IMPORTANT TO USE
THE COOL-OFF PERIOD
CONSTRUCTIVELY'

MYTH 7

YOU SHOULDN'T GO TO BED ANGRY

*Provocative Truth: Cooling off before addressing
a conflict can lead to better resolutions*

I think the main reason this myth persists so stubbornly is that people believe that, if you leave conflict unresolved, even overnight, it means you're going to damage your relationship. This is completely false. Forcing a quick resolution in the moment most likely means that it is not going to be thought out and it's potentially going to be insincere. Not only does this have the potential to leave you disgruntled, there is a good chance that you'll exacerbate the conflict.

I see this on *Married at First Sight* all the time. The participants are tired and frustrated late at night, so they're more impatient and less considered in their responses and actions, which inevitably makes the conflict worse. This, in turn, leads to more emotional strain around the idea that you have to resolve the disagreement with your partner regardless of whether you are ready to or not, which can create resentment.

This need for resolution in the moment is mirrored by many TV programmes. If a show is thirty minutes long, the conflict is nearly always resolved by the end. Unless it's an ongoing drama series, which might utilise a cliffhanger, TV shows tend to be contained, which creates an expectation in people that resolution is necessary in the moment. But that's not the way it works in real life. I also think that this notion of not going to bed angry is something that has been passed down from generation to generation. For example, I remember a pastor telling me and Jill this around the time that we got married.

As I've mentioned, I have recently been watching *Young Sheldon* with my kids. There is a scene in one episode in which Sheldon's mother and father are having an argument in bed, and Sheldon's mother says, 'Let's talk about it. I don't want to go to sleep angry.' It's this sort of thing that reinforces the myth. Similarly, the idea that you need to kiss and make up that is taught to us as kids, particularly when playing sports, also contributes to the sense that you need to have resolution in the moment. There would be some sort of issue and we'd be told to shake hands and make up. But nothing had actually been resolved. Instead, the issue had been swept under the rug — 'Just go past it and get it taken care of.' But that approach is not productive to anyone in the long run.

TAKING A PAUSE

It is very difficult, if not impossible, to regulate your emotions when you're angry. In a study run by the University of Massachusetts Amherst, the researchers showed people distressing images and then gave them the option to go to sleep or stay up.[1] When the people who chose to go to sleep awoke, the researchers showed both groups the distressing images again and found that those who had slept were much better at processing what they were seeing. In other words, emotional regulation requires rest. Your emotional reactivity is going to be lower when you have that rest, and the cooldown period means that you'll have less emotionally charged discussions, which is what you want in a conflict situation.

In addition to undermining the myth that you should never go to sleep angry, it is also fair to say that conflict resolution at any time of the day is going to be much harder if you are angry and don't take a step back to emotionally regulate. Another study, this time at Ohio State University, looked at the level of aggression in participants who were provoked by the experimenter and then asked to respond immediately or after a brief delay.[2] They found that after the short delay, the likelihood of an aggressive response was reduced.

Another study found that married couples who took short breaks during heated arguments reported having higher satisfaction and better resolution outcomes than those who didn't.[3] The breaks allowed the couples to calm down, reducing the intensity of the conflicts and facilitating more effective dialogue.

However, taking a pause is not enough on its own − it is important to use the cool-off period constructively. Going to bed and resting is a good use of that time. If the conflict happens during the day, letting the argument fester, ruminating over it and getting yourself more lathered up is a bad use of that cooldown time. Instead, you need to be able to regulate your emotions during that break.

Another example of an ineffective break is when one partner storms off without warning and goes to do something else. The person remaining is left thinking, 'Are you coming back? Are we ever going to talk about this?' Then, when they do come back, they more often than not say they don't want to talk about the issue any longer, and the conflict escalates again or is left unresolved. So, there's definitely a procedure to an effective cooling off.

HOW TO IMPLEMENT AN EFFECTIVE COOL-OFF PERIOD

The first thing you need to do is establish with your partner ahead of time that you will institute cool-off periods if a conflict escalates and is getting heated. Second, you and your partner need to know roughly how long the cool-off period is going to be, or it needs to be negotiated in the moment: 'How about we take thirty minutes?' Or: 'How about we sleep on this and deal with it tomorrow morning?' Whatever it may be, there's an agreed-upon time, and you and your partner therefore have a shared expectation that you will be coming back to focus on the problem again at that point.

Next, you need to carefully think about the scenario during the pause. That is how you will do most justice to the argument. This could be thinking about it from the perspective of your partner, or thinking about what your feelings are in this situation and how those feelings are impacting your thoughts. In other words, thoughtfully and purposefully applying your mind to what's happening, rather than stewing on it or not thinking about it all.

Next, you both need to follow through by coming back at the agreed-upon time and focusing just on the immediate issue at hand. This is the number one problem I see when couples come back together. During their break, they've gone away and thought about the ten other times their partner did the thing they're arguing about. It's like they've loaded up on ammo and are now going to mow their partner down. Yes, there could be a precedent for what's happening now, but just concentrate on the one thing and try to resolve that, as opposed to bringing up these ten other examples that might not even be entirely relevant anyway.

Finally, you need to develop your skills to the point that you can come away with a satisfactory resolution at the end. This could take a number of forms. Perhaps the resolution is that you heard each other out on this one but are going to agree to disagree. Maybe it's one thing that you're each going to do differently next time. Or it could be that you don't have an answer, but you're at least going to approach things differently in the future. Whatever it might be, having that agreed-upon resolution is vital after the cool-off period. If you are able to do all of that, it shows your strength and maturity as a couple.

Another way of looking at it is that, after the cooldown period, you're not coming to try to win the argument. You're coming to resolve the conflict in a way that you can both move forward. And you're trying to understand the conflict, as opposed to reacting to it. Just the understanding could be a satisfactory resolution.

MANAGING ANGER

Some people might think that because I'm advocating for a cool-off period, I'm suggesting that anger is a dangerous quality to be avoided at all costs, but that's not what I'm saying. Anger is inevitable and, in the right context, it is a useful human emotion. For example, it can be a sign of passion, interest and connection, and you can be angry and productive at the same time. It's therefore how you recognise and use anger that is important.

Anger is an emotion, and feelings are how we interpret our emotions. So, for some people, anger might result in extreme Incredible Hulk – type outbursts, whereas other people might acknowledge their anger and become curious as to what it means. That's one way in which relationships can make us so much better as human beings – they give us the opportunity to grow and rewire what we learned as children, so instead of becoming angry and throwing our toys out of the pram, we instead seek to understand what our anger signifies. How we interpret the emotion is the key.

You need to have the self-awareness to recognise when anger arrives and use it as a warning that the situation could escalate further if you allow yourselves to continue down this path, but if you take a break and go to bed or have a cool-off period, you can come back together and be constructive again.

There may be times when your partner is so angry that they don't want to engage in a cool-off period – 'I want to handle this now!' – but if you as a couple have worked on putting these processes in place, and you've built resilience, and you've established safety and emotional intimacy, then your partner is much more likely to agree to sleep on it or take a pause. It might take a number of attempts to get to that point, but your persistence will pay off, whereas if you haven't done any of that work, and you're dealing with a partner who is angry and doesn't want to cool off, you'll be stuck in an unhealthy cycle that becomes increasingly difficult to break.

SELF-GUIDED INTERVENTION: MASTERING THE ART OF SLEEPING ON AN ARGUMENT

OBJECTIVE

To understand and implement the practice of 'sleeping on an argument' as a tool for conflict resolution and relationship building, enhancing discipline, resilience and other essential relationship skills.

INTRODUCTION

Challenging this myth and offering such a simple piece of advice as sleeping on an argument can be beneficial is potentially incredibly impactful — it could even make or break a relationship. In fact, looking back over my fifteen years of working with couples, I think it is one of the single most important interventions I suggest, because it tests your discipline, your resilience, and so many other things. At the same time, it helps you to build the skills you need to have a successful relationship.

We can also begin to see that we're building on and utilising some of the skills that we've been talking about in previous chapters; for example, effective conflict resolution and the embracing of doubts. In terms of the latter, you might be a bit worried about what's going to happen after the cooldown period, but if you have embraced doubts in your relationship, then you'll be able to navigate your anxiety in this sort of scenario more successfully. This intervention tests your discipline and resilience while helping you develop crucial skills for a successful relationship.

I. UNDERSTAND THE CONCEPT

- Recognise that not all conflicts need immediate resolution. Taking a break can provide time to process emotions and gain perspective.
- Understand that 'sleeping on an argument' means agreeing to pause the discussion and revisit it after a designated period, usually the next day.

2. THE SCIENCE BEHIND IT

- Sleep helps in processing emotions and improving decision-making. Studies have shown that taking time away from a heated discussion can lead to more constructive outcomes.[4]
- Cooling down can reduce stress and anxiety, allowing for a more rational and calm approach to resolving the conflict.

3. CONNECT TO PREVIOUS SKILLS

- Use effective conflict resolution skills such as active listening (see page 32), empathy and clear communication after a cooldown period.
- Embrace doubts by acknowledging and managing any anxiety about what might happen after the cooldown period.

4. STEP-BY-STEP EXERCISE – CONFLICT SCENARIO

1. **Identify a conflict**
   - Think about a recent argument or an ongoing issue in your relationship.
2. **Agree to pause**
   - Communicate with your partner about pausing the discussion. Agree on a specific time to revisit the conversation, ideally after a good night's sleep.

- Example: 'I think we both need some time to cool down and think about this. Let's revisit this conversation tomorrow morning.'

3. Cooldown period
- During the cooldown period, focus on calming activities such as deep breathing, journaling or taking a relaxing walk.
- Reflect on your feelings and the core issues of the argument without dwelling on anger or blame.

4. Resume the conversation
- At the agreed-upon time, come back to the discussion with a calmer mindset.
- Use effective communication techniques: listen actively, speak calmly and be open to your partner's perspective.

5. REFLECT ON THE EXPERIENCE

- After resolving the conflict, reflect on the process. Consider the benefits of the cooldown period and any challenges you both faced.
- Discuss with your partner how this practice can be integrated into future conflicts.

6. PRACTICAL TIPS FOR SUCCESS

- Agree on a signal or phrase to use when initiating a cooldown period. For example, one partner might say, 'I need a minute to clear my head,' or simply raise a hand as a non-verbal cue, signalling that it's time to pause the conversation and step away for a moment to cool off before continuing the discussion.
- Ensure both of you are committed to revisiting the discussion at the agreed time.
- Practise self-care and stress management techniques during the cooldown.

7. COMMON CHALLENGES AND SOLUTIONS

- Challenge: Anxiety about unresolved issues.
  - » Solution: Remind yourself that the break is temporary and necessary for a healthier resolution.
- Challenge: One partner is unwilling to pause.
  - » Solution: Discuss the benefits of this practice and agree to try it as an experiment.

CONCLUSION

By integrating the practice of 'sleeping on an argument' you can enhance your ability to manage conflicts effectively, embrace uncertainties and strengthen your relationship. This self-guided intervention not only teaches the theory, but also provides practical steps to make this practice a natural part of your relationship toolkit.

TAKEAWAY

The next time you're in a heated discussion, consider pausing, allowing emotions to settle and revisiting the conversation with a clearer mind. It might just be the key to turning conflict into an opportunity for growth.

'MERELY LIVING
TOGETHER DOES
NOT NECESSARILY
TRANSLATE INTO
LONG-TERM
COMMITMENT'

MYTH 8

LIVING TOGETHER BEFORE YOU COMMIT PREDICTS LONG-TERM COMPATIBILITY

Provocative Truth: Long-term success comes from intentional commitment, not just living together

I think most people believe that when you live together you can begin to understand the other person's behaviours, and how and why they show up, and as such you can test out the relationship before committing long term. You could think of it a bit like a trial run: 'Let's just practise and act like it's the real thing and see what happens.' And the ultimate purpose of this is to reduce the risk of splitting up further down the line. This is why I think the idea that you should live together before you commit long term has become so pervasive as to have almost become a sacred relationship truth.

This is part of a huge cultural shift in the past decades that has seen the numbers of people cohabiting increase dramatically. For the baby boomer and earlier generations, it was considered unacceptable to live together out of wedlock. Whereas from Generation X onwards, unmarried couples living together has become the norm, contributing to a sense that it is a necessary step on the path to long-term commitment.

However, the reality is that most couples who end up cohabiting do not do so with intentionality from the outset. Often it comes down to an economic or practical consideration, and people slide into living together rather than really deciding to do so. In other words, they are not methodical or deliberate about the decision.

As of 2019, the National Center for Family and Marriage Research showed that the average time from the start of a romantic relationship to cohabitation in the USA was seventeen months.[1] For low socio-economic and education groups it was six to twelve months, whereas it was eighteen to twenty-four for people in higher categories. The reason for this discrepancy is in large part due to less necessity on the part of the latter group. In terms of Maslow's hierarchy of needs (see page 10), if you're towards the lower levels of the pyramid, it makes sense that you might need to go ahead and live with someone today, whereas if you're higher up the pyramid, with more of your basic needs satisfied, you have more space to make these kinds of decisions.

A study showed that well-educated and financially stable couples often cohabit later, even beyond the average of eighteen months, because these couples have the means to maintain separate residences until they feel ready for a significant commitment, which goes back to the key point of determination and intentionality.[2] According to another study, in opposite-sex relationships, men move into the female partner's residence approximately 25–35 per cent of the time, the woman moves into the man's home in 40–50 per cent of cases, and between 20 and 30 per cent buy a new home together.[3] So that was 2024. However, looking at the trend, women moving into men's homes is projected to decline to 30–40 per cent by 2030, and men moving into women's homes is projected to increase to 35–45 per cent, with 30–35 per cent buying places together. That's another massive cultural shift. It is supported by Tinder's Green Flag study, which found that 75 per cent of men are open to dating a woman who makes more money than they do.[4]

I think the increase in the number of people who are choosing to buy somewhere together could potentially be a sign that more people are making an intentional decision to live together, rather than sliding into it, and as such, cohabitation as a marker of long-term commitment could improve in the future. In the past, marriage was the primary marker of commitment, followed by having a child. Today, I think we're beginning to see that a conscious financial decision such as buying or renting a home together is becoming an elevated marker of commitment and intentionality.

SLIDING VERSUS DECIDING

One of the issues of believing in this myth is, perhaps counter-intuitively, to do with commitment. Some people think that moving in together signals that their commitment to the relationship is fully established. However, merely living together does not necessarily translate into long-term commitment. In my experience, it is not uncommon for one partner in a relationship to want to get married and the other to say, 'Marriage is just a piece of paper. We already live together, so we don't need to do it.' As a result, there is an element of ambiguity about the status of the relationship, as well as a discrepancy in their expectations.

Research shows that unmarried couples who cohabit and then slide into marriage versus making a deliberate decision have less satisfaction and higher divorce rates on average. The attitude in this type of scenario seems to be 'We're already living together, we have a child, we might as well just get married.' There is no real intentionality around committing to be together. And if you slide into a long-term relationship in this way, that's when you end up with lower satisfaction and higher divorce rates.

This has been labelled the 'cohabitation effect', which shows that couples who live together before marriage have a higher likelihood of divorce and lower marital satisfaction compared to those who don't.[5] But the distinction is intentionality. It's not that they're cohabiting per se; it's that they slid into the cohabitation and there was no intentionality behind the decision.

It seems like people think that if they've moved in together, they've reached the highest level of commitment, but in actual fact, without making a conscious decision that they want to be together in the long term, whether or not that means marriage or some other type of relationship model, they have missed an important step. And the consequence of this is that people are often left feeling stuck. Having a house with rent or a mortgage and bills to pay anchors you down. Having children, if you have any, anchors you down. Being part of the local community via the activities you do anchors you down. It's easy to see why some people therefore say, 'Let's just get married' or, 'Let's just stay together', without doing so because they really want to.

INTENTIONAL DECISION-MAKING

In *Find Love*, I wrote that it is important to be intentional about what you want and who you want in your life. It's no different once you are in a relationship. Couples who make deliberate decisions about their future together versus sliding into it have stronger, more resilient partnerships. Focusing on communication and conflict resolution also leads to stronger commitment, which in turn leads to more clarity, stability and trust in the relationship. And if you intentionally decided on the direction of your relationship, you'll likely have better value alignment as well. If you have shared values, you'll typically build a stronger foundation for your relationship.

There's a communication element here and being clear about what your goals are. If there is an imbalance of expectations, and one person thinks that moving in together signals sufficient commitment whereas the other person thinks it's a step towards something else, you're going to have a problem.

In my opinion, many of the unhelpful ideas about relationships stem from bestselling books that were written in the 1990s, and the promotion of living together first as a vital component of long-term relationship success is no different. The content from these books still lingers in the ether today. So, for example, in *Men Are from Mars, Women Are from Venus*, John Gray endorses cohabitation because he argues that living together can help partners understand and manage their differences before marriage. In *The Rules*, which had a huge impact on the dating landscape, Ellen Fein and Sherrie Schneider advise women to use cohabitation as a strategic tool to test compatibility and readiness for marriage, which is an extension of their philosophy that you constantly have to evaluate your partner before you commit to them. Even John Gottman, who has done a huge amount of positive work on how to maintain a healthy relationship, wrote about the link between cohabitation and marriage stability in his book *The Seven Principles for Making Marriage Work*, although his perspective was more balanced, pointing out the challenges as well as the benefits. On the plus side, he wrote that cohabiting couples can practise effective communication and conflict resolution skills.

There are, of course, benefits to living with someone, as you do get to know a person better in that situation. So, I'm not saying that cohabitation is bad in and of itself — it's purely down to intentionality. For example, there are certainly economic benefits to living together, as it allows couples to share expenses and save money, easing the pressures associated with individual financial burdens, but I think Gottman had it right: there are pros and cons, and you need intentionality if you are going to overcome those downsides.

Gottman's point that living together gives you the opportunity to practise some of the skills needed to have a successful relationship harkens back to Chapter 2, where we talked about the fact that you need to invite conflict into your relationship in order to learn how to navigate it and therefore grow as a couple.

PRIORITISING YOUR COMMITMENT

Jill and I were cohabiting before we decided to get married, but after we got engaged, we intentionally decided to stop living together. I don't know what you would call that — 'conscious decohabiting'? The reason for this was so that when we moved back in together, it would feel more special and unique. We were doing premarital counselling at that time and had both bought into the notion that we didn't want to slide into marriage or for it to feel run of the mill or mundane. We really wanted it to feel fresh, and for our married life to get started on the strongest footing. Ultimately, I suppose, the intention was to have a stronger relationship in the long term, and to make a conscious decision about being together. By making that sacrifice in the run-up to our wedding, we were also prioritising the commitment we were making to one another.

I recognise that it was quite a drastic move in some ways, and it's not something that every couple would necessarily want or be able to do. There may be financial or other commitments that would prevent you from living apart for a period of time. The main point I'm making, though, is that you need to consciously decide to commit and not just fall into it.

I also realise that we were in a privileged position. I had done a stint in investment banking, and I was in the process of launching a company. As such, I was already establishing myself as a professional, with some of the trappings of success that go along with that, including a nice car and an apartment in a converted tobacco warehouse that I loved. But I gave all of that up and moved into a spare bedroom in my aunt and uncle's house, and Jill moved back home with her parents. We did this because we couldn't afford to run two properties — even with the financial security that we were starting to build, we were still benefiting from sharing the bills for only one household. And we moved hours and hours apart, so we could only see each other every other weekend or so. You might be wondering why we put ourselves through all of that strain and turmoil. Well, I think it is generally accepted that what we most desire in life requires compromise, but I also think it requires sacrifice. And the question is, 'What are you willing to sacrifice for what you most desire?'

Jill and I lived apart for about a year before our wedding, but my gut tells me that any period in which you are able to go through a suitable period of reflection and re-evaluation is valuable. Whatever the length of time, it is helpful if you can free yourself from the things that might otherwise anchor you down while living together, as those things can be detrimental to you making the best decision. For example, one study found that couples who take the deliberate step of moving apart temporarily before marriage report higher levels of marital satisfaction and stability.[6] This period allows for reflection and re-evaluation of the relationship leading to more intentional decision-making, and applies just as much to long-term commitment as it does to marriage. Another study, meanwhile, found that couples who consciously decide to recommit by living apart before getting married are more likely to enter marriage with a clearer sense of purpose and commitment.[7]

♥

Cohabitation before marriage often feels like a practical 'trial run', but research shows that sliding into living together without clear intentions can actually lead to lower satisfaction and higher divorce rates. True compatibility is built through conscious decision-making, not just shared space.

SELF-GUIDED INTERVENTION: CREATING A RELATIONSHIP VISION BOARD AND EXPLORING TEMPORARY SEPARATION

OBJECTIVE

To enhance relationship alignment and satisfaction by creating a relationship vision board and considering the benefits of temporary separation before a long-term commitment or marriage.

INTRODUCTION

Creating a relationship vision board and exploring a period of temporary separation before marriage or long-term commitment can significantly impact your relationship's trajectory. This intervention fosters intentionality, clarity and alignment, ultimately contributing to higher levels of relationship satisfaction and stability.

PART I: CREATING A RELATIONSHIP VISION BOARD

I. UNDERSTAND THE CONCEPT

- A relationship vision board is a visual representation of your shared goals, dreams and values as a couple. It helps align your visions for the future and strengthens your commitment to mutual goals.

2. GATHER MATERIALS

- Collect magazines, newspapers, printed images, glue, scissors and a large piece of poster board or corkboard.
- Alternatively, you can use digital tools to create an online vision board.

3. REFLECT ON YOUR RELATIONSHIP GOALS

- Individually, take some time to reflect on what you want for your relationship. Consider aspects like career, family, travel, personal growth and shared hobbies.
- Write down your thoughts and aspirations.

4. SHARE AND DISCUSS

- Come together and share your individual reflections.
- Discuss your goals and aspirations, identifying common themes and areas of alignment.

5. CREATE THE VISION BOARD

- Select images, words and symbols that represent your shared goals and values.
- Arrange and glue these items onto the poster board, creating a visual collage of your relationship vision.

6. DISPLAY AND REVISIT

- Place the vision board somewhere visible in your home.
- Regularly revisit and update the board as your relationship evolves and new goals emerge.

PART 2: EXPLORING TEMPORARY SEPARATION

I. UNDERSTAND THE CONCEPT

- Temporary separation before a long-term commitment or marriage allows for individual reflection and re-evaluation of the relationship, and leads to higher levels of marital satisfaction and stability.

2. EVALUATE YOUR READINESS

- Discuss with your partner the possibility of a temporary separation.
- Assess your readiness and willingness to undergo this period for the benefit of your relationship.

3. PLAN THE SEPARATION

- Decide on the duration of the separation. While the length can vary, a period that allows for meaningful reflection is recommended.

- Determine the logistics: living arrangements, financial responsibilities and communication guidelines.

4. REFLECT INDIVIDUALLY

- Use the separation period to reflect on your personal goals, values and desires.
- Consider how these align with your relationship goals and whether there are areas that need adjustment or compromise.

5. SCHEDULE REGULAR CHECK-INS

- Schedule regular check-ins with your partner to discuss your reflections and feelings.
- Use these conversations to maintain a connection and ensure that the separation is constructive.

6. RE-EVALUATE AND RECOMMIT

- At the end of the separation period, come together to discuss your individual reflections and insights.
- Decide whether to recommit to the relationship with a clearer sense of purpose and intentionality.

CONCLUSION

By creating a relationship vision board and considering temporary separation, you can foster intentionality, clarity and alignment in your relationship.

TAKEAWAY

Embrace the power of visualising your shared future and the benefits of temporary separation to gain a deeper understanding of your relationship. These practices can help you build a more intentional, committed and fulfilling partnership.

'THE BOTTOM LINE
IS THAT BEING
ATTRACTED TO
PEOPLE IS A
FUNDAMENTAL
PART OF BEING
HUMAN'

MYTH 9

TRUE LOVE MEANS NEVER FEELING ATTRACTED TO SOMEONE ELSE

Provocative Truth: Attraction outside the relationship is natural, and being honest about these feelings can deepen trust and strengthen your partnership

I can see people coming at me on this one and it causing a lot of debate, as I think the myth that you should never be attracted to anyone else if you are in a relationship is one that is particularly entrenched in our culture. One of the main reasons for this is that it is heavily reinforced by the narratives that love is all-consuming and you should only have eyes for your partner, stemming from fairy tales and romantic movies and all of the other depictions of so-called perfect love. There's also a societal norm, especially in the West, stretching back to the creation of the nuclear family, that romantic partnership means total exclusivity, although that expectation was directed only at women until midway through the twentieth century.

An extension of this is the idealisation of monogamy in society and the concept that exclusivity of attraction is somehow related to moral integrity. And this myth also stems from the jealousy and insecurity that come from thinking that your partner is attracted to someone else. I know this is something I had to grapple with during the early days of my relationship with Jill.

It's worth saying from the outset that we are not just talking about physical attraction — we are also talking about emotional and sexual attraction too. Physical attraction is the appreciation of someone's physical traits — 'I love that person's legs,' for example. Sexual attraction is thinking about all of the things you'd like to do to those legs. Emotional attraction is different; it is the deep connection and appreciation you feel for someone's inner qualities, values and personality. It's about being drawn to how they make you feel, how they see the world and who they are as a person. With that being the case, and with us now wanting our partners to fulfil all of our needs, and vice versa, you can see how jealousy and insecurity could develop if you think your partner finds someone else particularly interesting, or inspiring, or sexy.

This expectation works both ways, with individuals thinking that their partners should never be attracted to anyone else, but also that they themselves shouldn't be either. This can lead to feelings of guilt and shame, which can, in turn, lead to emotional distress. Not admitting to being attracted to others creates a communication barrier that reduces your ability to engage in the kind of conflict that allows you to develop the skills needed to strengthen your relationship. It can also lead to you holding on to unrealistic expectations, which can then cause even further disappointment. If you learn five or ten years down the road that your partner is sometimes attracted to other people, the level of disappointment is going to be that much greater, because you've been harbouring this unrealistic expectation. And last, studies have shown that when you suppress feelings for an extended period of time, it not only leads to emotional strain but also begins to shift behaviour.[1] This is where you can see secretive actions and infidelity creep in, because the partner has been led to think that their attraction for others is wrong, but they can no longer suppress their feelings and so act upon them.

IT'S NATURAL TO BE ATTRACTED TO OTHER PEOPLE

The bottom line is that being attracted to people is a fundamental part of being human. So, the expectation should not be that you or your partner are never attracted to anyone else; it should be that you do not act upon that attraction in some way, unless that falls within the previously agreed boundaries of your relationship.

One study found that 70 per cent of women in committed relationships acknowledge feeling some level of attraction — emotional, physical or sexual — towards people other than their partners, and I wouldn't be surprised if the other 30 per cent were reporting inaccurately.[2] In other words, the majority of people in relationships feel attraction to others at some point, further emphasising just how normal this is.

The question is not therefore what you should do if you or your partner feel attraction towards other people — instead, it is determining at what point that attraction becomes a problem. The simple answer to this is that if the intensity of the attraction is such that it significantly influences your thoughts and behaviours, it has probably crossed the threshold of standard attraction to others that we all feel on a regular basis and some sort of intervention is necessary. The first element of this is the emotional impact that feeling guilty or anxious about your attraction can have if you sense that it is not right and it's weighing on you. The second part of this is behavioural change and interacting differently with either the person you're attracted to or your partner — for example, if you find yourself hiding interactions with the other person. Both of these things can affect your intimacy and emotional connection with your partner, which is when some sort of action is required.

NORMALISING ATTRACTION TO OTHERS

So, there are real downsides if you're seriously attracted to someone other than your partner but you're not articulating it. There is also a significant impact if your partner is intensely attracted to someone else, particularly if you're not aware of it and it has reached the level where it is influencing your partner's behaviour. This is when you are at risk of internalising the situation and believing that you are the problem, with all of the associated stress that puts on you. I have seen this a lot in my work with couples. One partner often begins to detect a subtle shift in the relationship dynamic. This change can be hard to put your finger on. Sometimes it is a feeling of distance and coldness, which can be easily chalked up to stress and the pressures of daily life. This is particularly the case if your partner is still coming home and giving you a kiss, and you're still having the occasional date night and going on holiday together. There's a continued level of normalcy in the relationship, yet there's also a chill. Perhaps the frequency of sex decreases. Or maybe your ability to communicate and resolve conflict lessens. Sometimes there's a complete avoidance of conflict in these scenarios, which gives the false impression that everything is OK, when, in fact, there is an underlying issue that needs to be addressed.

It is not uncommon in a situation like this for you to think that there is a problem in your relationship or that you are somehow to blame for your partner's apparent waning interest, only for you to find out that it is the other person's intensity of attraction that has led to the change in behaviour. This is when you can find yourself blindsided by the revelation that your partner has strong feelings for someone else, or, in extreme cases, a request to separate.

An outcome like this can be avoided. First, by an open conversation around attraction towards others, and second, by an early intervention if that attraction becomes more intense. This would save you from walking around on eggshells, feeling confused by what is happening in your relationship, and the inevitable turmoil that comes with that. It is more difficult to navigate a situation like this the longer it has been allowed to percolate without being addressed.

So, you can avoid attraction to others jeopardising your relationship by avoiding it escalating to a damaging point, but also by normalising it from the outset. After all, as we've seen, attraction to others is the rule, not the exception. And it doesn't mean that you or your partner don't love one another or don't want to be in a relationship. Yes, it might be an uncomfortable topic to discuss, but uncomfortable conversations ultimately strengthen relationships. Your communication is stronger and more efficient, there's more honesty in the partnership and you can work through insecurities and jealousies when they are at a low level, rather than after two years when your partner wants to go off with someone else. This is a common theme throughout the book: you have to go through low-level challenges to be able to learn the skills to navigate them if they worsen, or avoid them getting to that stage in the first place.

SELF-GUIDED INTERVENTION: NORMALISING ATTRACTION TO OTHERS AND STRENGTHENING COMMUNICATION

OBJECTIVE

To normalise the discussion of attraction to others in your relationship and strengthen communication, thereby enhancing trust, emotional clarity and relationship satisfaction.

INTRODUCTION

Normalising attraction to others and fostering open communication are crucial steps in building a secure and strong relationship. Even those with an insecure attachment style can achieve secure attachment through consistent, effective communication, which fosters trust, emotional safety and a deeper connection in the relationship. Over time, this helps individuals feel more secure and supported, gradually reshaping their attachment patterns. This intervention will show you how to navigate attraction to others in an effective way.

I. UNDERSTAND THE CONCEPT

- Acknowledge that attraction to others is a normal human experience. Communicating openly about these feelings can prevent misunderstandings and strengthen your relationship.
- Early implementation of this practice can make it easier to maintain a healthy dialogue throughout your relationship.

2. NORMALISE ATTRACTION TO OTHERS

- Begin by discussing your attraction to celebrities or people you don't know personally. This can make the topic feel less threatening and more casual.
- Example: 'I think Hugh Jackman is really attractive.' Or, 'I think Beyoncé is hot.' Make it light-hearted and fun to help you to ease into the conversation.

3. ASSESS THE INTENSITY OF THE ATTRACTION

- If either of you feels that your attraction to someone else has become problematic, assess the intensity of these feelings.
- Consider whether the attraction is having an impact on your thoughts and behaviours and therefore affecting the relationship or causing distress.

4. CHOOSE YOUR COMMUNICATION METHOD

- Writing a letter:
  - » Write a letter to your partner expressing your feelings and experiences related to the attraction.
  - » Benefit: Allows for self-reflection and thoughtful expression. Your partner can read and process the information in their own time.
- Direct conversation:
  - » Have a face-to-face conversation in a neutral, safe space.
  - » Benefit: Immediate feedback and dialogue.

5. STEPS FOR WRITING A LETTER

- Start with a positive affirmation of your relationship and your commitment to each other.
- Clearly express your feelings about the attraction, emphasising that it doesn't diminish your love for your partner.
- Suggest ways to address and navigate these feelings together.
- Example: 'I wanted to share something with you because I believe in our open communication. Lately, I've found myself attracted to someone else, and it made me realise how much I value our relationship. I think it's important for us to talk about it and find a way to navigate this together.'

6. STEPS FOR DIRECT CONVERSATION

- Choose a calm and neutral setting where both of you feel safe.
- Begin with a positive statement about your relationship.
- Express your feelings honestly but gently.
- Allow your partner to respond and discuss ways to address the issue together.
- Example: 'I've noticed that I've been feeling attracted to some-one else, and I wanted to talk to you about it because I value our relationship and believe in our open communication.'

7. WHAT TO ADDRESS IN YOUR LETTER OR CONVERSATION

- Normalise the experience: Start by acknowledging that feeling attraction outside the relationship is a natural human experience. Reassure your partner that discussing it openly will strengthen your bond by fostering honesty and mutual understanding.
- Set boundaries together: Have a conversation about what both of you consider appropriate boundaries when it comes to external attractions. Agreeing on mutual expectations can reduce anxiety and enhance trust in the relationship.
- Focus on reconnection: Use the letter or discussion as an opportunity to explore ways to reconnect and deepen intimacy in your relationship. Engaging in new, shared experiences can reignite your bond and help both partners feel valued.

8. SCHEDULE REGULAR CHECK-INS

- After the initial conversation or letter, schedule regular check-ins to maintain open communication on this issue.
- Discuss your feelings, any changes and ways to continue supporting one another.
- Example: 'Let's talk again in a week to see how we're both feeling and if there's anything we need to address.'

9. CONTINUE COMMUNICATION AND REFLECTION

- Regularly revisit and reflect on your communication practices.
- Use expressive writing or conversation as tools for ongoing emotional clarity and connection.
- Studies show that couples who maintain open communication report improvements in trust and satisfaction over time.

CONCLUSION

By normalising attraction to others and fostering open communication, you can build a more secure, trusting and satisfying relationship. This self-guided intervention provides practical steps to enhance your relationship through honest dialogue and consistent effort.

THE INTERVENTION IN PRACTICE

When it comes to the normalisation of attraction to others in your relationship, this can be achieved in part by expressing attraction for people you don't know, such as celebrities. I know, for example, that Jill loves Spike Lee and Idris Elba — she'd drop me in a second for either of them. I was a bit jealous at first, but now it is so normalised that we have fun with it, and whenever I give her a gift, it's always from Idris.

TAKEAWAY

Remember, the key to a strong and secure relationship lies in normalising and openly discussing your feelings. By doing so, you can navigate challenges together and build a deeper, more resilient connection.

'THE NEED FOR EQUITY
IN A RELATIONSHIP
THEREFORE APPLIES AS
MUCH TO THE FINANCIAL
ASPECT OF IT AS IT DOES
TO THE DIVISION
OF LABOUR'

MYTH 10

LOVE CAN OVERCOME ALL FINANCIAL OBSTACLES

Provocative Truth: Love alone can't solve financial problems – successful relationships need financial compatibility and clear, shared money management

An extension of our earlier discussion around the myth that love should be unconditional is that it should also be able to overcome any obstacle, including financial difficulties. The prevailing attitude seems to be that money is a materialistic consideration, and it should not get in the way of true love. I think this is in part to do with wider issues around discussing money in society. Many people still seem to think that it is a private, taboo subject, even at a time when we are seeing a trend towards meatier topics being addressed in a dating and relationships context. In the early days of my matchmaking agency, you weren't even supposed to ask someone who they voted for, whereas today people are willing to go deep into potentially controversial topics from the outset. Today, many of us are willing to have sex with someone right out of the gate, but we're still not willing to talk about our finances. This keeps money and love separate in people's minds.

There also seems to be a sense for some people that finances are inconsequential to romantic bliss, as well as a widespread idealistic view of love, reinforced by popular culture, that love is an all-conquering force. This is arguably indicative of a wider lack of acknowledgement that relationships happen within a practical, real-world context and require work. And your financial situation is a key contributor to that reality.

A study by Policygenius[1] found that only 37 per cent of couples discuss their financial situation before moving in together, and Trust Bank (formerly SunTrust) in the USA conducted some research in which they found that only 51 per cent of couples discussed their finances before getting engaged, and that this lack of communication often kept going after marriage.[2] Meanwhile, Wells Fargo, another US bank, did a survey that found that 77 per cent of married couples discussed their finances at least monthly. On the surface, that seems like a large percentage, but that doesn't sound often enough to me, and it also means that almost a quarter are not talking about finances at all, which blows my mind.

THE DOWNSIDES OF FINANCIAL SECRECY

There are a number of consequences to not being upfront about your finances or thinking that they are somehow separate from your relationship. Perhaps the most obvious one is that financial strain can lead to significant stress, which can, in turn, put pressure on your relationship, especially if you are hiding something. In fact, financial strain is one of the top five leading causes of divorce, although I would argue that it's more the inability to resolve the conflict that arises from financial difficulty that actually leads to relationships breaking down.[3]

Another outcome of thinking that money and love should be kept separate is that when financial problems inevitably arise, you're not equipped to handle them because you haven't developed any of the necessary communication or conflict resolution skills. It also points to a tendency to avoid critical discussions, which can lead to significant misunderstandings and ruptures – for example, when someone hides debt from their partner. It seems to me that one of the main reasons that relationships don't survive financial difficulties is because they often come as a huge shock to one partner, with one person having gone off and done something that the other had no idea was happening. So, if you avoid having that difficult discussion and debt is eventually uncovered, the consequences are going to be greater as a result of it showing up later. And it can also lead to a situation of dependency on one side and resentment on the other, with one partner feeling overburdened and the other feeling reliant. The need for equity in a relationship therefore applies as much to the financial aspect of it as it does to the division of labour. This does not mean that both people have to contribute the same amount of money to the relationship – just that there needs to be transparency and a sense of agreed fairness.

The majority of Americans are carrying debt and have low credit scores.[4] So, if you have been a strong financial steward of your money and highly disciplined as you build towards financial stability, then you fall in love with someone who is carrying a massive debt load or terrible credit, this can have a significant impact on your relationship. And not just because of the money difficulties themselves. Good people sometimes get themselves into terrible situations, but poor financial management can also be indicative of a pattern of behaviour that you should at least be aware of if you are preparing to commit to someone in the long term. It should be a point of consideration in your assessment of compatibility with that person, as it speaks to quite divergent values when it comes to money. You're not necessarily on the same page if you don't have that discussion up front.

If you are open about money and see a strong financial footing as being important to the health and strength of your relationship, you get reduced stress, enhanced trust, improved communication, superior conflict resolution and better alignment of goals and values. You are also more likely to be able to get to a position of financial stability, which improves feelings of security. So, there are many upsides to seeing finances as being intrinsic to romantic partnership rather than inconsequential or separate from it.

SINGLE OR JOINT ACCOUNTS?

The predominant trend in relationships today is for each partner to manage their own finances separately but also to have a joint account that both people contribute to. However, studies show that this is not the optimal way.[5] The best financial set-up in a relationship is to have a joint account only and combine your finances. There are a number of reasons why people don't do this. Most of our relationships with money stem from what we were taught by our parents when we were young. If you grew up in a lower socio-economic household, you might think first and foremost about making ends meet, whereas if you came from a wealthier background, your default position is more likely to be how you leverage or spend your money. Whatever your background, there is a bias towards keeping control of your own funds.

But what the studies ultimately bear out is that when you fully join your finances together, it requires you to have open communication, and it is this dialogue that creates increased strength. That's why studies on this subject suggest that having a joint bank account leads to higher satisfaction in the relationship, and maintaining separate bank accounts results in lower satisfaction rates. But it's not because of the banking situation at the end of the day — it's because of the level of communication and conflict resolution that is required if you have one account. If you have separate accounts and contribute to a shared pot of money or a joint account, you will probably not need to have as many hard conversations about your finances. The opposite is true if you only have a joint account. Jill and I only have a shared account, and it leads to us having discussions about the allocation of money on an almost daily basis.

I am a great admirer of businessman and Plymouth Argyle owner Simon Hallett, who has done a lot to turn around the fortunes of the football club since taking over in 2018. Jill and I were recently listening to him being interviewed on a podcast, and he relayed a conversation he'd had with his wife around the time of the purchase in which he'd said something like, 'I'm thinking about buying a football team,' and she'd replied, 'You're thinking about buying it or you already have?' He'd then had to admit to her that he'd already gone ahead. Now, I don't know how he and his wife choose to manage their finances, and his decision to buy a football team without first discussing it with her could be indicative of the level of trust they have built up in one another, but when Jill and I listened to the podcast we were surprised that he had made such a big financial decision without consulting her first. While the majority of us are not making financial decisions on that level, I would argue that it is still extremely important for us to have open dialogue around our purchases and full transparency when it comes to money. And you can achieve that kind of communication and transparency regardless of your banking situation if you are completely open about your finances at all times.

If you are transparent about money, you'll be in a better position to overcome financial hardship should it come, because you'll have the skills to be able to discuss it. What I often see happening in relationships is that when financial difficulties arise, people's first response is, 'How can I resolve this myself?' But the beauty of having a partner is that you have someone to have the discussion with who can help you to emotionally regulate in the moment of stress and share some of the burden.

From a practical standpoint, if you have separate accounts, I'd recommend setting up at least one shared account so you can begin to co-manage and commingle some funds. I think that's a very strong first step to financial transparency. But even though the research reveals the benefits of having a single joint account, I wouldn't necessarily want to advocate that everyone adopt that approach. The reality is that some people will have selected the wrong partner, and having a joint account with the wrong partner could be disastrous. However, at the very least, you should be aware of what's happening with the finances in your relationship. I'm finding more and more that many women in particular cannot leave their bad relationships because they feel financially trapped. A way to mitigate this is to have a joint account in addition to your own account so that you have an overview of the money situation at all times. Beyond that, it is about having regular conversations about your finances.

The simplest bit of advice I can give you is that you need to have the money conversation early on, and it is best if you can establish full financial transparency from the beginning of your relationship. However, if you're reading this book and you're part of the majority who entered a long-term relationship without having a proper discussion with your partner about money, you need to have that conversation now.

SELF-GUIDED INTERVENTION: FOSTERING FINANCIAL COMPATIBILITY AND COMMUNICATION IN RELATIONSHIPS

OBJECTIVE

To recognise that love alone cannot overcome financial challenges in a relationship. Successful relationships require financial compatibility, open communication about money and effective money management to thrive.

INTRODUCTION

Finances are one of the most common sources of stress in relationships, yet many couples avoid having open conversations about money. Establishing financial transparency early on — or as soon as possible — is key to creating a successful and stable partnership. This intervention will help you and your partner foster financial transparency and create a foundation for long-term financial success and satisfaction. The steps will guide you through discussing financial expectations, managing money as a team and ensuring financial compatibility.

PART I: STARTING WITH FINANCIAL TRANSPARENCY

I. HAVE THE MONEY CONVERSATION EARLY ON

- Whether you're just starting your relationship or have been together for years, it's crucial to have an open and honest conversation about your finances. Financial transparency helps prevent misunderstandings and fosters trust between partners.
- If you haven't had this conversation yet, now is the time. Acknowledge that discussing finances might be uncomfortable, but it's essential for the health of your relationship.
- Example: 'I realise we haven't really talked in detail about our finances yet. Let's sit down and discuss where we both stand, what our financial goals are and how we can work together.'

2. ESTABLISH FULL FINANCIAL TRANSPARENCY

- Financial transparency means being completely open about your current financial situation — this includes income, savings, debts, spending habits and financial obligations. Both of you should lay everything out on the table to ensure there are no surprises later on.
- Example: Share information about your bank accounts, credit card debt and financial obligations (for example, student loans or family support). 'Here's where I'm at financially. I want us to be on the same page moving forward.'

3. DISCUSS FINANCIAL EXPECTATIONS

- Clarify your financial goals and expectations with each other. Do you have the same priorities when it comes to saving, spending and investing? Discuss your short- and long-term financial goals to ensure you're both working towards a common future.
- Example: 'What are your thoughts on saving for a home or retirement? Are there any financial goals that are really important to you?'

PART 2: ESTABLISHING FINANCIAL COMPATIBILITY

I. ACKNOWLEDGE DIFFERENT FINANCIAL THRESHOLDS

- It's important to recognise that everyone has a different threshold for financial comfort. What bothers one of you might not bother the other, and it takes humility to accept and respect those differences.
- Example: One of you might be more comfortable with risk, while the other prefers to save conservatively. 'I know I'm more relaxed about spending, but I realise that makes you feel anxious. Let's figure out a compromise.'

2. DISCUSS SPENDING AND SAVING HABITS

- You and your partner likely have different spending and saving habits. Discuss these differences openly and decide how to manage finances together in a way that respects both of your habits and needs.
- Example: 'I tend to spend on small things, while you like to save for bigger purchases. How can we balance our different styles?'

3. FIND A FINANCIAL SYSTEM THAT WORKS FOR BOTH OF YOU

- Some couples combine all their finances, while others keep separate accounts. There's no one-size-fits-all approach, but it's important to find a system that works for both you and your partner. Whether you choose joint accounts, separate accounts or a mix of both, agree on a strategy that aligns with your financial goals.

- Example: 'Would you feel more comfortable if we had a joint account for shared expenses but kept our personal spending separate?'

PART 3: MANAGING MONEY AS A TEAM
I. SCHEDULE REGULAR FINANCIAL CHECK-INS

- Just as you would schedule relationship check-ins, it's important to have regular financial check-ins as well. Use these meetings to review your financial goals, track your progress and adjust your spending or saving as needed.
- Example: Set aside time once a month to review your budget, check savings goals and discuss any upcoming expenses. 'Let's make sure we're still on track with our financial goals.'

2. APOLOGISE AND ADJUST WHEN NECESSARY

- If one of you makes a financial mistake or crosses a boundary, it's important to apologise sincerely. Financial mistakes can cause tension, but a well-placed apology can help defuse the situation. Research shows that couples who apologise to each other frequently have higher satisfaction (see the next chapter for more on this).
- Example: 'I'm really sorry I overspent on the credit card this month. I realise it's impacted our budget, and I'll do my best to be more mindful next time.'

3. CREATE A SAFE ENVIRONMENT FOR APOLOGIES

- When discussing finances or apologising for financial missteps, make sure you're in a calm and neutral environment. Apologies given in the wrong setting can lead to defensiveness or further conflict.

- Example: Choose a time when both of you are relaxed and not distracted by work or stress. 'Let's talk about our finances after dinner when we can both focus and discuss things calmly.'

4. SHARE FINANCIAL RESPONSIBILITIES

- Managing money as a team means sharing financial responsibilities. Divide tasks such as budgeting, paying bills and tracking expenses. This ensures that both of you are equally involved in managing the household's finances.
- Example: One of you can handle tracking the budget, while the other manages investments or savings goals. 'Let's divide up our financial tasks so we're both involved in managing our money.'

PART 4: BUILDING FINANCIAL RESILIENCE AS A COUPLE

I. FOCUS ON LONG-TERM FINANCIAL GOALS

- While daily spending habits are important, your focus as a couple should be on long-term financial goals. Work together to create a plan for your future, whether that involves saving for a home, planning for retirement or building an emergency fund.
- Example: 'Let's set a goal to save for a down payment on a house within the next five years. How much do we need to save monthly to reach that goal?'

2. BUILD FINANCIAL TRUST AND COMPATIBILITY OVER TIME

- Financial compatibility doesn't happen overnight. It takes time, communication and adjustments as your financial situation and goals evolve. Regularly revisiting your financial plan helps build trust and ensures that both you and your partner feel secure in the relationship.
- Example: Check in every few months to make sure you're both still comfortable with your financial arrangement and make adjustments if necessary. 'Are you still feeling good about how we're managing our finances? Should we make any changes?'

3. BE PATIENT AND COMPASSIONATE

- Financial issues can cause stress, but it's important to be patient and compassionate with your partner. Financial compatibility is built through open communication, respect for each other's differences and working together to find solutions.
- Example: If one of you is struggling with financial stress, be supportive rather than critical. 'I know it's been a tough month financially. Let's figure out how we can make things easier for both of us.'

CONCLUSION

Financial compatibility and open communication are key to a successful relationship. Love alone cannot overcome financial challenges, but by having honest conversations about money, establishing financial transparency and working together as a team, you can build a strong financial foundation and avoid common financial pitfalls.

TAKEAWAY

Finances are a crucial part of any relationship, and successful couples prioritise open communication, transparency and mutual respect when it comes to money. By scheduling financial check-ins, discussing your financial goals and supporting each other through challenges, you and your partner can achieve financial compatibility and strengthen your relationship in the process.

'THE HIGHEST-
SATISFACTION
COUPLES APOLOGISE
TO ONE ANOTHER ON
AVERAGE ONCE A WEEK'

MYTH 11

APOLOGIES ARE NOT
NECESSARY IN A GOOD
RELATIONSHIP

Provocative Truth: Apologies heal and strengthen relationships,
as they foster humility and open communication

It always amazes me when I hear couples say that they are so close that they don't ever need to apologise to one another. To me, this suggests a lack of depth in their relationships and minimal emotional intelligence. Because the provocative truth is that couples who apologise frequently and effectively have substantially higher satisfaction in their relationships than those who don't.

Again, the source of this myth is in part down to culture. People tend to apologise more in collectivist societies, such as Japan, South Korea and China, primarily because of the societal traditions of respect in those countries, whereas people apologise less in more individualistic countries, such as Germany, Russia and Finland. There are also gender differences when it comes to apologising.[1] We all have a different threshold around what we perceive to be apology-worthy situations, and there are often imbalances in relationships whereby one partner has a lower threshold than the other; unfortunately, it tends to be more gender based.[2] Research shows that men generally have a higher threshold for what they consider to be offensive behaviour and therefore believe their actions are less often worthy of an apology.[3] In these situations, the partner who has the higher threshold for what is apology-worthy expects the partner with a lower threshold to meet their standards: 'It's unnecessary to have to apologise for my tone of voice, because that's just the way I was brought up.' Or, 'That's the way it is in my culture, so why should I have to apologise? Just suck it up.' However, the more effective strategy is to lower your threshold and be more empathetic.

People also seem to feel that if they are in a successful relationship, there'll be nothing to apologise for in the first place. They seem to think that being in love means existing in a state of bliss. But this is a false expectation, as this level of perfection in which nothing apology-worthy ever happens doesn't exist.

AN APOLOGY IS A
CONFLICT RESOLUTION TOOL

Some of the downsides of believing this myth include increased tension in the relationship, especially if you are actively avoiding an apology, and the emotional distance that comes from a situation in which there is a reluctance to apologise. Also, if you are one of those higher-threshold people and you are not apologising, and your partner is witnessing that, there is likely to be an erosion of trust. Overall, the most important reason for an apology is to resolve conflict and get to that place where you're strengthening your conflict resolution, so without the apologies, there's unresolved conflict.

You might expect that the person who needs to apologise often knows deep down that they should but doesn't want to take personal responsibility, and refusing to apologise is an attempt to mask their agency in the issue that's arisen. I certainly used to think that was the case more often than not; however, over time,

I've come to believe that this is actually the exception rather than the rule and most people are unaware that they are doing things that are worthy of an apology. Yes, most people are conscious of the large situational apologies and, in my experience, that seems to be the standard way that couples approach apologising — something big happens and there's a significant outbreak of emotion followed by a considerable sense of embarrassment and guilt that leads to an apology, or at least the awareness that there should be an apology if one is not immediately forthcoming. But I also think that most people don't realise how often they could or should be apologising for everyday infractions. To that point, studies suggest that the couples who report the highest levels of satisfaction tend to apologise weekly.[4] When I read this, it led to me asking Jill how often I apologised to her, and she estimated about six times a year. So, if you're looking at the level of frequency that makes a difference, I think most of us, myself included, are missing it.

WHEN TO APOLOGISE

It is not uncommon for there to be an imbalance in the thresholds of when an apology is merited between two people in a relationship. If that is the case, and one person doesn't apologise very often and has a higher threshold, the partner with the lower threshold will likely have given up looking for apologies and won't say when their threshold has been met. In this kind of situation, there needs to be some sort of proactive communication in order to tease this out. I see this in my own relationship. I'm sure Jill is often thinking, *I'm not going to tell him for the 500th time!* So, it is on the part of both partners to go after that information.

So, what sort of action or situation should necessitate an apology? Well, it depends, because the key is whatever is offensive to your partner, and there is no floor to that. It's also highly subjective. That's why being plugged in and empathetic is so important, and why you need strong communication skills. Drawing on your emotional awareness and emotional intelligence, you will begin to understand what constitutes a situation in which you have caused your partner to feel uncomfortable, disrespected, embarrassed and so on, and that you should apologise as a result of that. It takes a certain level of humility to accept that your partner's threshold is different from yours and that the things that bother them are valid. It also requires emotional stability, open-mindedness and kindness, as these traits contribute to someone's willingness to apologise.

I would therefore encourage people to understand and adjust their threshold when it comes to making apologies. The first step is being empathetic and really trying to understand your partner's perspective. Actively listen and pay close attention to them, communicate well and take time for self-reflection.

As I mentioned, the studies tell us that the highest-satisfaction couples apologise to one another on average once a week. Now, I'm not advocating for you to manufacture reasons to apologise or to say sorry unnecessarily, but I do think there is value in ensuring your antenna is up and you are more aware of whether or not you have met your partner's threshold for an apology. Even if you do not notice anything, being more aware will lead to you being more empathetic. It's an area I know that I could work on. I need to put my antenna up to help me detect occasions when I am missing or overlooking that an apology would have been welcomed.

Attachment style also has a big role to play here. Individuals with a secure attachment style are more likely to offer sincere, effective apologies, because they're more emotionally regulated. A study in the *Journal of Social and Personal Relationships* found that insecurely attached and anxious people will sometimes apologise even more frequently than securely attached people, but these apologies are less effective because they are apologising based on fear of rejection or abandonment.[5] Apologising is also a great way to earn a more secure attachment in your relationship, as it builds trust and helps to make your partner feel safe. But it's quality over quantity. If you feel like you are apologising all the time, then try to assess what is driving that. Is it fear? Is it embarrassment? Is it indicative of an insecure attachment? So, beyond the frequency of apologies, it's also their effectiveness that is important.

EFFECTIVE VERSUS INEFFECTIVE APOLOGIES

Studies show that effective apologies are more associated with people with higher well-being. Yes, apologies reduce stress, which improves well-being, but individuals who frequently and effectively apologise typically have higher well-being in the first place. The other traits associated with people who tend to apologise well are empathy and conscientiousness. And cultural orientation also plays a large role here.

An Ohio State University study on apologies found that only 50 per cent of couples offered comprehensive and effective apologies, which means there is a huge number of people out there who need to learn how to apologise well.[6]

An effective apology begins with acknowledging the wrongdoing by recognising it and stating what your role was. This incorporates an understanding of the situation and the part you played. Next is an expression of remorse, whereby you show genuine regret for the harm that was caused. And you need a commitment to make amends, specifically indicating how you will prevent the issue from reoccurring and how you will make up for the mistake.

In addition, and this touches upon our discussion of conflict resolution, you need to make sure that you are in a safe environment before making an apology, otherwise it might not land. And you have to be aware of your body language as well. You could do everything right on paper — acknowledge your wrongdoing, express remorse and promise to make amends — but if you do so without looking at your partner, or with your phone in your hand, it will completely undermine the apology. This speaks to the importance of executing the apology well.

If you do all of that, and apologise effectively, you will build a track record, almost like making a deposit in a bank account, which fosters and increases trust. This means that the next time you apologise, there'll be a greater willingness to listen and accept what's being said. And your relationship satisfaction will increase because of that trust. It therefore makes sense that the couples with the highest satisfaction are constantly apologising to one another. It's a way to continually strengthen the infrastructure of your relationship, and a very effective but simple tool to bring about mutual growth and develop the relationship to the highest level, because you're constantly trying to understand what the other person wants and needs. In the process, you are more likely to find that your needs and wants are met too.

SELF-GUIDED INTERVENTION: APOLOGISING TO HEAL AND STRENGTHEN YOUR RELATIONSHIP

OBJECTIVE

To help you understand the value of apologies in strengthening your relationship, improving emotional connection and building greater trust.

INTRODUCTION

Apologies are a key part of maintaining a healthy, strong relationship, though they are often undervalued or overlooked. In my own relationship, I've spent a lot of time working on this area, and I'll be using examples of that work to illustrate how effective apologies can improve communication, deepen emotional connection and strengthen the bond between partners. This intervention will guide you through understanding your own and your partner's 'apology thresholds', developing the habit of regular, sincere apologies and fostering a healthier, more empathetic relationship dynamic, thus enhancing relationship satisfaction.

PART I: UNDERSTANDING YOUR APOLOGY THRESHOLD

1. RECOGNISE THE IMPORTANCE OF APOLOGIES

- Apologies are essential in maintaining humility, kindness and respect within a relationship. Apologising doesn't mean weakness; it shows a willingness to take responsibility and repair emotional damage.
- Example: 'I realise I may have been a bit short with you earlier. I'm sorry for not being more patient.'

2. WORK OUT YOUR OWN APOLOGY THRESHOLD

- Reflect on your behaviour to understand how often you feel it's necessary to apologise. Are there moments when you overlook the need for an apology because it seems too small? Understanding your own threshold for apologies is the first step to improving communication and emotional intelligence.
- Example: Spend a week observing your behaviour and asking yourself if an apology would have been warranted in certain situations. 'I snapped at Jill when I was stressed but didn't apologise — was that something that merited an apology?'

3. DECIDE IF YOU SHOULD ADJUST YOUR THRESHOLD

- Once you've assessed your apology threshold, consider whether it would benefit your relationship to lower it. Apologising more frequently for minor missteps can prevent resentment from building up and help your partner feel seen and respected.
- Example: If you don't often apologise for minor frustrations, make an effort to acknowledge those moments, even if they seem small.

PART 2: UNDERSTANDING YOUR PARTNER'S
APOLOGY THRESHOLD

I. OBSERVE AND LEARN YOUR PARTNER'S THRESHOLD

- Figuring out your partner's apology threshold can be trickier, but it's crucial for developing greater emotional intelligence and empathy. Pay attention to how your partner reacts in different situations and whether they seem upset or hurt, even if no major conflict occurred.
- Example: 'I noticed Jill seemed distant after our conversation earlier. Did I miss something that warranted an apology?'

2. ENGAGE IN OPEN COMMUNICATION

- Talk to your partner about their feelings on apologies. Some people may feel satisfied with fewer apologies, while others appreciate frequent acknowledgement of small missteps. Understanding their needs will help you tailor your responses.
- Example: 'I've been thinking about how often we apologise to one another. Do you feel like I acknowledge mistakes when they happen, or are there times when you wish I'd said something?'

3. TEST THE WATERS WITH A WEEK OF MINDFUL OBSERVATION

- For one week, be mindful of your partner's reactions and whether you've missed opportunities to apologise. This doesn't mean looking for reasons to apologise where none are needed, but becoming more aware of subtle cues that may indicate hurt feelings or frustration.
- Example: 'This week, I'll make a note of any moments where I think Jill might have expected an apology, even if I didn't initially think one was needed.'

PART 3: APOLOGISING EFFECTIVELY AND BUILDING THE HABIT

I. APOLOGISE SINCERELY AND SPECIFICALLY

- Make sure your apologies are sincere and specific. A general 'I'm sorry' might not carry the weight your partner needs. Acknowledge exactly what you're apologising for and show empathy for how it affected your partner.
- Example: 'I'm really sorry for interrupting you during dinner. I didn't mean to shut down the conversation, and I can see how that might have frustrated you.'

2. PRACTISE HUMILITY AND OPENNESS

- Apologies require humility and acceptance that your partner's feelings are valid, even if you didn't intend to cause harm. Being open to your partner's perspective and willing to make amends strengthens trust.
- Example: 'I didn't realise my tone came across as dismissive. I'm sorry for that — I'll try to be more mindful next time.'

3. USE APOLOGIES AS A TOOL FOR EMOTIONAL GROWTH

- Regularly apologising not only repairs small emotional fractures, but also helps you to grow emotionally. It builds empathy, emotional awareness and kindness, leading to a stronger connection.
- Example: 'I've noticed that when I apologise quickly, it prevents small frustrations from building up, and I feel more connected to Jill afterwards.'

4. BUILD THE HABIT OF APOLOGISING WEEKLY

- Research shows that the most satisfied couples apologise at least once a week. By aiming for frequent, thoughtful apologies, you can maintain a healthier dynamic and avoid letting small issues build up over time.

- Example: Set a reminder for yourself to reflect on the past week's interactions and whether any moments could benefit from an apology. This habit will keep you tuned in to your partner's needs.

CONCLUSION

Apologies are not a sign of weakness; they are a powerful tool in maintaining a healthy, emotionally intelligent relationship. By understanding your own and your partner's apology thresholds, practising humility and making regular apologies a habit, you can strengthen your relationship and deepen emotional intimacy.

THE INTERVENTION IN PRACTICE

Realising that this was something I should probably try myself, I spent a week observing my behaviour and noting when an apology to Jill would have been merited. As a result, I noticed a few times when I was short with her because of work stress or impatience. For example, during dinner one evening, I was preoccupied with my phone and responded dismissively to something she said. I didn't think much of it at the time, but later I realised that Jill seemed quieter than usual. I hadn't been fully present, and my tone had probably come across as unkind. The next morning, I apologised: 'I'm sorry for being distracted during dinner last night. I wasn't really listening, and I think my tone came across as dismissive. That wasn't my intention, and I'll be more mindful next time.' Jill appreciated the acknowledgement, and we had a great conversation about the importance of being present. From this experience, I learned how often small things can be overlooked. By spending the week paying attention to missed opportunities for apologies, I became more aware of how important it is to stay emotionally connected. Now, I try to build that awareness into my daily life, apologising when needed and maintaining a strong connection between us.

TAKEAWAY

Don't wait for major conflicts to apologise. Make it a habit to recognise and address the small moments that may require acknowledgement. Apologising frequently and sincerely strengthens emotional bonds, prevents resentment and fosters greater connection and empathy within your relationship.

'BELIEVING THAT
PASSION WILL
INEVITABLY FADE CAN
CREATE EMOTIONAL
DISTANCE'

MYTH 12

PASSION WILL INEVITABLY FADE

*Provocative Truth: Passion and intimacy don't
have to fade; they can be sustained and even
deepen, growing stronger over time*

My hunch is that this is one of the myths in the book that most people are going to think is the truth. But before I explain why it is, in fact, a myth, I think it's important that I first define what I mean by passion. I previously mentioned psychologist Robert Sternberg's triangular theory of love consisting of intimacy, commitment and passion. Passion by his definition is characterised by 'the drives that lead to romance, physical attraction, sexual consummation, and related phenomena in loving relationships'.[1] But he also says that the three components are interlinked, so passion also has hints of intimacy and commitment.

WHAT IS PASSION?

As I interpret it, passion isn't necessarily the output. It's the drive. It's the desire. It's the want. I say all the time, and I think some people think it's just a line, that I feel more intense love for Jill today, twenty-plus years in (which makes me feel old that we've been together for that amount of time) than I did when we were first going out. And that intensity is characterised by a desire to be close. Let's just sit on the couch together. Let's do something together, whatever it may be. It's not a case of passionately kissing at the bus stop, although that was never really us in the first place. There is probably less physicality today than back then, but overall the passion, informed by commitment and intimacy, is higher.

Beyond this, I think what people actually mean when they say that passion fades is that infatuation fades. And that is more often than not true, which is no bad thing, as being infatuated is not a good recipe for a healthy relationship in the long term. Infatuation can feel like an intense attraction, which can of course feel exciting, but really it is an unhealthy idealisation of a partner, leading to obsessive thoughts and a sense of urgency that you need to have high levels of emotional and physical arousal at all times. That's often what you see when you see intense love characterised in film and on TV. But, again, that is not what I interpret real and sustainable passion to be.

Infatuation is short-lived and fades quickly; passion can be sustained and nurtured over a long period of time. Infatuation lacks any significant emotional connection; passion is characterised by a deep emotional bond. Infatuation leads to obsessive behaviours and irrational decisions. I see this all the time when a person does something they wouldn't normally do, supposedly because of how in love they are. But it's not love; it's infatuation. Passion, on the other hand, leads to positive behaviours and healthy, supportive interactions. And passion doesn't have to fade if you work at it. In fact, if you have selected a strong partner, and you're doing all the things that I advise in this book, passion can grow over time.

In a landmark study on the topic of sustained passion, highly respected researchers in the field of psychology looked at a group of people who reported still feeling intense love for their partners after being together for 21.4 years on average.[2] When they scanned these people's brains in an MRI while showing them pictures of their loved ones, along with pictures of other people — some they knew and some they didn't — they found that the majority of the participants exhibited the same signs of intense love for their partners as would normally be associated with new love. This clearly demonstrates that passion does not inevitably fade. Yes, it might fade without work, but it doesn't *inevitably* fade. Passion may also evolve or change over time, but that is not the same as it diminishing in strength. It is just going to look different in year five, or fifteen, or twenty, than it does in year one.

Once again, it is largely culture that dictates what a lot of us think passion should look like. But television and other forms of media, including some of the projects I've been involved with over the years, do a poor job of differentiating passion from infatuation or obsession, which ultimately does us a disservice when it comes to what we should be aspiring to in our relationships. I think this is reinforced if we look at previous generations — our parents' or grandparents', say — and judge the passion in their relationships on these terms. We might then think that the passion in our own relationships is going to go the same way. But the passion in their relationships hadn't necessarily dwindled — it had just developed or changed.

That said, as we've explored, there were different expectations for many people when they were entering long-term relationships in the past, and passion wasn't always a key driver. That doesn't necessarily mean their satisfaction levels were lower, though — in fact, by some measures, the relationship satisfaction of the baby boomers was higher overall. Again, the reason for this, according to Eli Finkel, was that they required less from their relationships, and there wasn't the same requirement as there is today for a partner to fulfil all our needs.[3] The expectations we place on our relationships have gone through the roof since then, including this false idea about what constitutes real and ongoing passion.

A SELF-FULFILLING PROPHECY

Believing that passion will inevitably fade can create emotional distance, which might look like avoiding deep conversations, becoming less affectionate or neglecting to share thoughts and feelings with your partner. This quiet distancing can erode the connection between partners long before any real problems arise, and sometimes functions a bit like a defence mechanism to help avoid hurt. This can lead to dissatisfaction with the relationship and increase the risk of infidelity, because you begin to think that you can only get the intense levels of passion that you believe to be associated with new relationships if you seek out someone different. There's also a sense of resignation and complacency that happens when you accept that the decline of intimacy is going to happen. But probably the most powerful outcome of believing that passion fades is that it becomes a self-fulfilling prophecy. You resign yourself to the fact that it's going to happen and withdraw from the relationship, which lessens the feeling of passion, which causes you to withdraw further, and so on.

I also think there's a widespread sense that people think passion should be automatic and easy — that it's all about chemistry. In actual fact, in order to maintain passion over the long term, you have to put effort into keeping it going. There's a unanimous feature of all couples who have strong satisfaction and high emotional intimacy: they do the work. They have great conflict resolution, because they have embraced conflict and worked through it. And they have lasting passion because they realised it was something that needed to be nurtured over time. It's also a repetitive process. The most successful couples are working on their relationships all the time, whether they realise it or not.

Understanding that passion and intimacy can stay the same and even grow over time brings with it many positive impacts. You get better emotional connection and higher overall relationship satisfaction, which is what you want. You also build greater resilience, and you can get increased sexual satisfaction. And, last but not least, you get personal growth.

♥

To reiterate, the three components of a successful long-term relationship are emotional intimacy, commitment and passion. However, because many people believe that passion will inevitably fade over time, they settle for emotional intimacy and a partner who sticks by them. But that's not enough. We need all three. And the beauty is that each one drives the next — they're all interrelated. If you do the work in this book, the passion in your relationship can develop and grow, becoming more meaningful over time and contributing to your own well-being, as well as a successful relationship.

SELF-GUIDED INTERVENTION: SUSTAINING PASSION OVER TIME

OBJECTIVE
To challenge the myth that passion inevitably fades in long-term relationships and to provide practical strategies for maintaining passion and intimacy.

INTRODUCTION
One of the most common misconceptions about long-term relationships is that passion will naturally diminish over time. However, passion doesn't have to fade — it evolves and can even deepen if nurtured properly. In this intervention, we'll explore how spending quality time together, introducing novelty and staying emotionally connected can keep passion alive. We'll also discuss how to navigate obstacles, such as the challenges of raising young children, and how to integrate these strategies into your everyday life.

PART I: UNDERSTANDING PASSION IN RELATIONSHIPS

I. PASSION IS MORE THAN INFATUATION

- Passion is not just about physical attraction or spontaneous displays of affection; it's the ongoing desire to be close, to connect and to share experiences with your partner. It evolves from the intense infatuation of early relationships into something deeper, informed by emotional intimacy and commitment.
- Example: 'Passion in our relationship looks different now than it did when we first started dating. We might not be kissing at every opportunity, but I still feel an intense desire to spend time together and stay emotionally connected.'

2. THE ROLE OF THE LOVE LANGUAGES

- The 'five love languages', a concept popularised by Dr Gary Chapman, offer a framework for understanding how people express and receive love: words of affirmation, quality time, physical touch, acts of service and receiving gifts.[4] While I am not generally an advocate of the love languages, quality time stands out as a key factor in sustaining passion.
- Example: 'Spending intentional, uninterrupted time together helps to nurture our connection and maintain the passion in our relationship.'

3. QUALITY TIME PROMOTES LASTING PASSION

- Passion is sustained by emotional intimacy, and quality time allows you and your partner to build and maintain that intimacy. When you spend time together without distractions, it fosters closeness, deepens your bond and helps you reconnect amid life's challenges.
- Example: 'We make it a point to have dinner together every night, without phones or TV, to focus on one another and our relationship.'

PART 2: OVERCOMING OBSTACLES TO SPENDING QUALITY TIME

I. THE CHALLENGE OF FINDING TIME

- One of the most common challenges couples face, especially those with young children, is finding time for each other. The demands of parenting or work can make it difficult to carve out moments for intimacy and connection.
- Example: 'We're both so exhausted after taking care of the kids all day, but we know we need to spend time together to stay connected.'

2. SUGGESTIONS FOR NAVIGATING THESE OBSTACLES

- Schedule 'mini dates': Even if you can't go out for a full date night, schedule short, intentional 'mini dates' at home. This could be as simple as having a quiet cup of tea together or watching a favourite show.
- Involve the kids: Find ways to integrate family activities that bring joy and connection for both of you. You can bond over shared moments as a family while also connecting as a couple.
- Use early mornings or late evenings: If it's hard to find time during the day, wake up early or stay up a little later to have quiet moments just for the two of you.
- Example: 'After the kids go to bed, we make it a habit to spend thirty minutes together just talking or planning our next weekend, even if we're tired.'

PART 3: THE POWER OF NOVELTY IN MAINTAINING PASSION

I. THE CONTRIBUTION OF NOVELTY

- Research shows that couples who engage in new activities together report higher levels of passion and relationship satisfaction. Novelty adds excitement and unpredictability to a relationship, stimulating feelings similar to the early stages of love.

- Example: 'We decided to try a new hobby together — cooking a dish we've never made before — and it was so much fun learning something new as a team.'

2. HOW NOVELTY KEEPS PASSION ALIVE

- Doing something new together activates the brain's reward system, much like when you first fell in love. These shared experiences help reignite feelings of excitement and curiosity, both of which are essential for sustaining passion.
- Example: 'Last weekend, we took a spontaneous day trip to a town we'd never been to. It felt like a mini adventure, and it brought us closer.'

3. SIMPLE WAYS TO INTRODUCE NOVELTY

- Try new activities together: Whether it's exploring a new hobby, visiting a place you've never been or cooking a different meal, novelty doesn't have to be complicated or expensive.
- Change up your routine: Even small changes, like switching up your regular date-night activity or taking a different walking route, can bring a sense of freshness to your relationship.
- Plan surprises: Occasionally surprising your partner with something thoughtful can break the monotony and bring back excitement.
- Example: 'We usually go to the same restaurant for date night, but last week I surprised my partner by taking us somewhere new. It felt like a fresh experience, and we had a great time.'

PART 4: SUSTAINING PASSION WITH GRATITUDE AND POSITIVE INTERACTIONS

1. PRACTISE DAILY EXPRESSIONS OF GRATITUDE

- Expressing gratitude regularly can help maintain emotional intimacy and passion. When you both feel appreciated, you are more likely to remain connected and passionate over time.

- Example: 'I've started thanking my partner every day for something they've done, whether it's making coffee or being a great parent.'

2. USE THE 'MAGIC RATIO'

- Dr John Gottman's research suggests that successful relationships have a ratio of five positive interactions for every negative one.[5] Positive interactions — such as compliments, small acts of kindness and physical affection — help counterbalance conflicts and keep the emotional climate of the relationship positive.
- Example: 'After a disagreement, I make a point to do something kind for my partner, like making their favourite meal or leaving a note of appreciation.'

3. MAKE TIME FOR PHYSICAL AFFECTION

- Physical touch is a key component of passion. Even non-sexual touch, like holding hands, hugging or cuddling, helps to reinforce the emotional bond and keep the flame alive.
- Example: 'We've started making time every morning for a long hug before we start the day — it's a simple way to feel connected.'

CONCLUSION

Passion in long-term relationships does not have to fade. By focusing on quality time, introducing novelty and expressing gratitude regularly, you can sustain emotional and physical intimacy over the years. It's about intentionally creating moments of connection and ensuring that both you and your partner feel valued and appreciated.

TAKEAWAY

Passion is not automatic — it requires effort and intentionality. By making time for your partner, trying new things together and nurturing emotional intimacy, you can keep the spark alive and ensure that your relationship continues to grow in depth and passion. Even amid life's challenges, such as raising young children or moving house, these small but consistent efforts can make a significant difference.

'OVERALL, I'M NOT
SAYING THAT VALUES
ARE NOT IMPORTANT.
I'M JUST SAYING THAT
THEY SHOULDN'T BE
THE PRIMARY FOCUS'

MYTH 13

SHARED VALUES ARE THE MOST IMPORTANT CRITERIA FOR A STRONG RELATIONSHIP

*Provocative Truth: Personal well-being before and during
a partnership is more important than shared values for
the ongoing success of a relationship*

One of the questions I most often ask people when discussing relationships is: 'Out of these four, which is the strongest predictor of a high-satisfaction relationship: sexual compatibility, shared humour, shared values or strong personal well-being?' And every single time, shared values is the top answer by far, to the point that many people look at me like it's absurd to even ask the question. This made me wonder if they were right, and why we are so fixated on values in the first place.

I think it stems, in essence, from the fact that our values express our beliefs about the most fundamental and important aspect of our lives — about family, finances, religion, politics. However, some people confuse interests with values. If you and your partner both like Taylor Swift, that's not a shared value — that's a shared interest. A value is a much broader category. One of your core values could be creative expression or a deep love of music, which leads to you having the shared interest in Taylor Swift.

If values speak to the most essential aspects of our lives, it makes sense that people would, in turn, believe that shared values are the best predictor of relationship success. But while this is undoubtedly a key factor, I do not believe it is the most important one. To me — and this is backed up by research — personal well-being is more important (more on which below).[1]

As with a lot of things in life, the promotion of values in relationships can be traced in large part back to religion and the notion of being equally yoked, which is a reference to oxen being tethered to one another when they are ploughing a field. Pastors and elders took this reference in the Bible and developed it to say that you need to be equally yoked in terms of sharing the same religion with the person you marry. This would lead to you having the shared values necessary to allow you to walk lockstep together and be more effective in how you go about life. This then became an important criterion that families would use to determine whether or not they would put two people together, because it was families who were mainly making that decision right up until the twentieth century. This was a key aspect of what anthropologist Joseph Henrich calls the 'Marriage and Family Plan', which was an effort during the Middle Ages to promote the growth of nuclear families over clans.[2] This also led to the entrenchment of the class system, which further cemented the importance of shared values in determining matches.

Today, a study by the Pew Research Center found that 47 per cent of married adults in the USA still believe that shared religious beliefs and values are key to the success of a marriage.[3] This statistic represents the impact of religious teachings and helps to explain why the perception that shared values are the most important aspect of a successful relationship has persisted over the years. And now the idea is perpetuated by relationship experts, who often misinterpret the research showing that values are incredibly important as meaning they are the *most* important thing. However, a Gottman Institute study from 2014 on marital stability and relationship dynamics showed that, while couples who believe in the importance of shared values often report lower conflict levels, this belief often masks underlying issues that are more significant predictors of relationship success, such as well-being.[4] So, even though there is research suggesting that values are important, it is not necessarily the only or best thing to focus on, and it can, in fact, lead to more important things being neglected.

VALUES ARE ONLY ONE COMPONENT OF COMPATIBILITY

I recently saw this fixation with values play itself out in my work life. I was discussing a feature with the producers of a new show, and we agreed that a compatibility test was going to be needed to determine which couples should be together and which shouldn't. When we returned to this feature at a subsequent meeting, it had been changed from 'compatibility test' to 'values test'. When I asked them if this was the compatibility test we had talked about previously, one of the producers replied, 'Yes, to find out if the couples are compatible, we need to test their values.' They had misunderstood what I had been telling them. Shared values is only one of the many things that go together to suggest good compatibility (as I discussed in more depth in *Find Love*).

In addition to the Gottman Institute study pointing out that the prioritisation of shared values can mask more important drivers behind the success of your relationship, there is also the potential to overemphasise similarity, which is something that a lot of people think they want. When Jill and I started our matchmaking agency, we would joke with one another (although there was a lot of truth in it) that people looking for heterosexual relationships were searching for a version of themselves with different sex organs. They wanted someone who was brought up the same way as them, was educated to the same level and liked the same things (in other words, had the same interests). They might even want something as specific as finding someone who loved pineapple on their pizza as much as they did. However, the truth of the matter is that as long as you have a strong sense of well-being and high self-esteem, you are equipped to be with almost anyone.

If you search for someone who is too similar to you, whatever type of relationship you are in, you can end up overlooking things like emotional intelligence and strong communication, because you don't need those things so much if you are with a version of yourself. Focusing too much on values can also lead to stagnation in a relationship, because it can create a sense that if you have shared values, you're perfect for one another and less effort is therefore needed to make the relationship work. And, last but not least, if you prioritise values, you're not prioritising the thing that is most critical, which is your and your partner's well-being.

It can also make things a little bit stale sometimes if you both want the same things. Where's the surprise coming from? Where's the novelty? You need a way to keep your relationship fresh and interesting. This is a little example, but if it weren't for Jill, I would never have realised how much I enjoy yoga. When she first suggested it, I thought, 'That's not for me — I'm not flexible enough for that.' But after giving it a try, I found that it really helped me relax and improved my focus. Now, it's something I look forward to doing regularly. It's a small example, but it shows how being open to a different perspective, even something simple like trying yoga, can lead to growth.

You do sometimes hear people say that opposites attract, suggesting that there is some sort of collective acknowledgement that similarity is not always the best thing, but I think most of us do not consider this to be a recipe for long-term relationship success. I think the prevailing idea is, in fact, that opposites attract and then attack. It's like being attracted to the bad boy or girl, but then thinking that's not necessarily the best thing for you. But actually, when you have strong well-being, the beauty is that you can work with almost anyone in the world, which is extremely empowering, and the different perspectives that you bring to the relationship can be a really good thing.

THE FUNDAMENTAL IMPORTANCE OF WELL-BEING

There are a number of studies that support well-being as being the fundamental aspect of a strong relationship. For example, one study found that psychological well-being is one of the strongest predictors of marital satisfaction.[5] (I think it's important to emphasise that we are equating satisfaction rather than longevity with a strong relationship — see Chapter 21 for more on this.) The researchers found that individuals who have better mental health reported higher marital satisfaction regardless of whether they shared values with their partner. The study showed that psychological well-being accounted for approximately 30 per cent of the variance in marital satisfaction, which emphasises that your well-being is key.

Another study looked at personality and individual differences, focusing on emotional intelligence, which is a component of personal well-being. It showed that couples with better emotional intelligence reported higher relationship satisfaction, and emotional intelligence was found to be a more robust predictor of relationship quality than shared values, accounting for 40 per cent of the variance in relationship satisfaction.[6]

A 2006 study found that partners who actively pursued personal growth also reported higher levels of marital satisfaction. The research revealed that personal growth accounted for 35 per cent of the variance in marital adjustment, which refers to how well partners adapt to and navigate the challenges of marriage, fostering a harmonious relationship.[7] Interestingly, shared values explained only 20 per cent of the variance, highlighting that personal development has a greater impact on marital satisfaction than simply having common beliefs or goals. This suggests that focusing on self-improvement can play a significant role in enhancing relationship quality.

And, last but not least, psychologists Ed Diener and Martin Seligman looked at the link between life satisfaction and relationship quality.[8] They found that higher life satisfaction, or greater well-being, was strongly correlated with positive relationship outcomes, including higher levels of happiness and lower levels of conflict. Life satisfaction accounted for 45 per cent of the variance in relationship quality, surpassing the influence of shared values. All of these studies underscore that elements of well-being are more important than shared values when it comes to successful relationships.

This again speaks to the ultimate goal of your relationship being about allowing you to be your best self. It all starts with you and where you are in life, whereas someone else's values matching with yours is external. In order for you to get the best relationship, you really need to think about how you're going to grow as a person.

VALUES CHANGE

I sometimes hear people say that values are constants, staying with you throughout your life, which is one of the reasons why people believe they are the most important foundation of a successful relationship; however, I don't necessarily think that's the case. With the abundance of information we have today, it makes sense that our opinions, which are informed by the new knowledge that we're acquiring, shift and change. It is no different for our beliefs and values. You could also argue that the greater your well-being, self-esteem, curiosity and so on, the more variance you'll have in your values. This is because greater self-awareness and emotional health allow you to explore diverse perspectives and be more open to new experiences, broadening the range of traits and principles you find meaningful. So, to primarily predicate your relationship on this platform that's constantly moving and shifting and evolving just doesn't make intellectual sense to me. With well-being, on the other hand, that's all you, and the more it grows, the more availability you will have for your relationship and the deeper connection you will have with your partner. Additionally, the more flexible you are, the more you're able to compromise and the better you're able to communicate, which, as I've said before, are really important skills and attributes in a good relationship.

The benefits of prioritising well-being over shared values as the core aspect of a successful relationship therefore include a deeper connection, personal growth, growth as a couple, adaptability and resilience, which is key in terms of being able to resolve conflict.

Overall, I'm not saying that values are not important. I'm just saying that they shouldn't be the primary focus and, actually, if you really want to strengthen your relationship, you should be thinking about how you can make yourself the best person possible, as this will have all these other knock-on effects in terms of a higher-satisfaction relationship, which is what we're all after.

SELF-GUIDED INTERVENTION: PRIORITISING PERSONAL WELL-BEING OVER SHARED VALUES IN RELATIONSHIPS

OBJECTIVE

To guide you in understanding that personal well-being, rather than shared values, is the key to sustaining a strong, fulfilling relationship.

INTRODUCTION

Many people believe that shared values are the cornerstone of a successful relationship, but research suggests that personal well-being is actually more important. While values do play a role, focusing too much on them can mean you overlook the factors that truly determine a strong relationship, such as emotional intelligence, resilience and personal growth. This intervention will help you to shift your focus from aligning on values to fostering personal growth, emotional intelligence and overall well-being as a means of enhancing relationship satisfaction. We'll explore how well-being influences relationship success, how values can change over time and how focusing on yourself can lead to a stronger partnership.

PART I: UNDERSTANDING THE ROLE OF WELL-BEING IN RELATIONSHIPS

I. THE PRIMACY OF PERSONAL WELL-BEING

- Personal well-being is one of the strongest predictors of relationship satisfaction. Studies show that individuals with better mental health, higher emotional intelligence and a commitment to personal growth report higher satisfaction in their relationships. When you focus on your well-being, you are better equipped to communicate, resolve conflicts and grow alongside your partner.
- Example: 'I prioritise my mental health and emotional well-being. When I feel good in myself, our relationship thrives.'

2. WELL-BEING OVER SHARED VALUES

- While shared values can help minimise conflict, they are not the strongest predictor of a happy relationship. Prioritising personal well-being ensures that you are in the best possible position to build a strong relationship, even if you and your partner don't agree on every value.

- Example: 'My partner and I don't always see eye to eye on certain issues, but because we both focus on self-care and emotional health, we're able to navigate those differences with understanding and respect.'

3. THE IMPACT OF EMOTIONAL INTELLIGENCE

- Emotional intelligence — the ability to understand and manage your own emotions and those of your partner — is a crucial component of personal well-being. Research shows that couples with higher emotional intelligence experience greater relationship satisfaction than those who only focus on shared values.
- Example: 'I've been working on becoming more aware of my emotions and how I respond to stress, and it's helped me communicate more clearly with my partner, leading to fewer arguments.'

PART 2: EMBRACING PERSONAL GROWTH FOR RELATIONSHIP SUCCESS

I. THE IMPORTANCE OF PERSONAL GROWTH

- Personal growth is a key factor in relationship satisfaction. Studies indicate that individuals who actively pursue personal development experience higher levels of marital satisfaction. This growth allows you to bring the best version of yourself to the relationship, which positively influences your partner.
- Example: 'I've started taking courses to improve my communication skills, and it's made a huge difference in how my partner and I resolve conflicts.'

2. GROWTH ENCOURAGES FLEXIBILITY AND ADAPTABILITY

- Personal growth helps you to become more adaptable and open to different perspectives, which can enrich your relationship. If you and your partner have different values, focusing on growth makes it easier to navigate those differences with empathy and flexibility.

- Example: 'Even though my partner and I have different opinions about finances, focusing on my personal growth has helped me become more open to finding compromise.'

3. WELL-BEING PROMOTES RESILIENCE

- When personal well-being is a priority, you become more resilient in the face of challenges. This resilience not only helps you to deal with personal struggles but also strengthens your relationship. Resilient individuals are better equipped to manage conflicts and bounce back from difficulties in their relationship.
- Example: 'When things get tough, I rely on the emotional resilience I've built through mindfulness and therapy. It's helped me to stay grounded and support my partner through challenging times.'

PART 3: RECOGNISING THE LIMITATIONS OF SHARED VALUES

I. VALUES ARE NOT FIXED

- Contrary to popular belief, values can change over time. As you grow and evolve, your priorities and beliefs may shift. This is why basing your relationship solely on shared values can lead to challenges later on. Personal well-being, on the other hand, is an internal quality that grows with you.
- Example: 'When we first got together, my partner and I valued the same things, but over time, our interests and priorities shifted. Thankfully, we both focused on our well-being, which kept us connected despite the changes.'

2. THE ROLE OF NOVELTY AND VARIETY

- Relying too heavily on shared values can make a relationship feel stagnant. Novelty and variety are important for keeping a relationship dynamic and engaging. Different perspectives and interests can bring excitement and growth to the partnership, preventing it from becoming stale.

- Example: 'I didn't think I'd enjoy yoga, but my partner convinced me to give it a try. Now, it's something we both do together, and it's brought a new layer of connection to our relationship.'

3. SIMILARITY ISN'T ALWAYS THE GOAL

- Many people think that being with someone similar to themselves will create a harmonious relationship. However, too much similarity can lead to complacency. It's important to be with someone who challenges you and brings new perspectives, fostering growth and keeping the relationship fresh.
- Example: 'My partner and I have different hobbies and interests, and while that seemed like a challenge at first, it's actually kept things interesting and allowed us both to grow.'

PART 4: SHIFTING THE FOCUS TO WELL-BEING

I. DEVELOP A PERSONAL WELL-BEING PLAN

- Start by identifying the areas of your life that contribute to your well-being: physical health, mental health, personal growth, emotional resilience and so on. Create a plan that focuses on improving these areas, knowing that, as you grow, your relationship will benefit.
- Example: 'I've made a commitment to regular exercise, meditation and journaling to improve my mental and physical well-being, and I've noticed that I bring a more positive energy to my relationship.'

2. PRACTISE SELF-CARE AND ENCOURAGE YOUR PARTNER TO DO THE SAME

- Self-care isn't selfish — it's essential for a healthy relationship. Encourage your partner to focus on their well-being as well, so that you're both bringing your best selves to the relationship.

- Example: 'Carving out time for self-care has helped me to be more patient and present, and I think it could do the same for you.'

3. BUILD EMOTIONAL INTELLIGENCE TOGETHER

- Working on emotional intelligence as a couple can improve communication, conflict resolution and overall satisfaction. Practise naming emotions, understanding each other's triggers and developing empathy for one another's experiences.
- Example: 'We've started having regular check-ins where we talk about our emotions and how we're feeling in the relationship. It's helped us become more in tune with each other.'

4. EXPLORE NEW INTERESTS TOGETHER

- Keep the relationship dynamic by exploring new activities or hobbies together. This adds variety, helps you to grow as a couple and strengthens your bond.
- Example: 'We decided to take a photography class together, and it's been a fun way to connect and try something new.'

CONCLUSION

While shared values are important, they are not the most crucial element of a successful relationship. Prioritising personal well-being — through emotional intelligence, personal growth and resilience — creates a stronger foundation for long-term happiness and fulfilment. As you grow individually, your relationship will naturally thrive, allowing you to navigate differences with empathy and understanding.

THE INTERVENTION IN PRACTICE

I know that accepting there's a whole other set of things that are much more important than our shared values was something of an epiphany for me. From a practical standpoint, how I previously looked at my relationship was that we had to prioritise and do things together that fit within our belief system. For example, I like hip-hop and Jill rock music, so I was of the opinion that we should go to music festivals together because we both enjoy music. But now, upon reflection, although that's nice, and, yes, you should prioritise spending time together, what's more important is my well-being and Jill's well-being going into those things. That's what we should be prioritising. For example, developing a skill and mastering our environment — anything that contributes in a positive way to Carol Ryff's six dimensions of well-being (see page 17) — is going to be much more impactful on the health of our relationship than trying to enact a shared value such as a love of music.

TAKEAWAY

Shift your focus from shared values to personal well-being. By developing emotional intelligence, embracing personal growth and fostering resilience, you create a relationship that can adapt and thrive, regardless of value differences. Strengthen yourself first, and your relationship will follow.

'CHILDREN EXPOSED
TO CONFLICT
ENVIRONMENTS
CAN SUFFER FROM
ANXIETY, DEPRESSION
AND BEHAVIOURAL
ISSUES'

MYTH 14

STAYING TOGETHER FOR THE KIDS IS MORE IMPORTANT THAN YOUR OWN HAPPINESS

Provocative Truth: A toxic or unhappy relationship is worse for your kids than separation

I hate to single out my mother again, but she once told me that you always stay together for the kids — the idea being that parents should remain in an unhappy or dysfunctional relationship because, by doing so, they are providing a stable environment for their children. The further implication of this is that divorce or separation causes more harm to a child than staying together in a bad relationship, despite the heightened conflict that may be occurring in the family home.

This myth is again steeped in religion, and there is a strong social and cultural aspect to it too. Many of us have been led to fear that the disruption of a separation will have a negative impact on a child that will lead to significant emotional distress. It's going to impact them in school academically and there are going to be social issues with their friends too. And some of this may be true — separations are hard on everyone involved. I have seen first-hand the social stress that can be imposed on a child whose parents are splitting up. It therefore makes sense that wanting to protect a child would often force people to stay in a broken relationship.

There are also strong societal expectations that promote the importance of the nuclear family and stigmatise separation and divorce, which makes people feel pressured to stay together for the sake of the family. I see it all the time with mothers in particular, who often tell me that they don't want to be single mums. Being a single parent is hard, so you can see why some people might be reluctant to choose that path. And then there's the personal guilt, with parents feeling like they should be sacrificing their own happiness for their children's.

However, research has shown that children exposed to conflict environments can suffer from anxiety, depression and behavioural issues.[1] As issues in a relationship typically stem from conflict, you can see how that would be exacerbated if parents stayed together beyond the breakdown of a relationship. It also models unhealthy behaviour, which children learn by observing their parents. If children are growing up in an environment where conflict or disrespect or unhappiness is prevalent, then this normalises that in their minds, and it teaches them unhealthy relationship dynamics. And then last, but definitely not least, is the parents' well-being. Staying in an unhealthy or even toxic relationship means stress, hurt and upset that impacts all aspects of their lives.

FOSTERING A HEALTHY ENVIRONMENT

Children thrive in a healthy, supportive environment, and if that means parents need to separate to create that space, then it's the best course of action. Such an environment can be created whether parents remain together or co-parent, as long as they model healthy relationship dynamics, either as a couple or as individuals. In other words, you can still provide a nurturing environment as co-parents if you're unhappy in the relationship, but staying together while masking unhappiness will likely create more stress, making it harder to sustain a positive atmosphere for your child.

A healthier, more supportive environment for your children means less conflict, and therefore less chance of anxiety, depression and behavioural issues. Parents modelling respectful and healthy relationship dynamics also means that their children are more likely to develop their own positive relationships in the future. And ending a relationship that is no longer working and creating high levels of conflict also results in parents who are happier, which has a positive impact on their well-being, allowing them to be more effective and present as parents.

All of this highlights why it's so important for parents to evaluate their relationships with each other, not just their relationships with their children, and decide if separation is the best path. Being aware of and understanding this is crucial. And this applies across all types of relationship-parenting models, not just heteronormative ones.

It's similar to when I shared a controversial post on my socials about how Jill and I prioritise our relationship first, because that's the foundation for providing a healthy and stable environment for our children. If we didn't prioritise our relationship and allowed issues to fester, those fractures would be magnified for our kids.

♥

I truly believe this is a generational issue. For previous generations, there was often a belief in staying together 'for the kids', but we are now beginning to recognise that unresolved conflict in a relationship can cause more harm than good, especially when children absorb unhealthy dynamics. That's why I feel it is so important to challenge this myth and prioritise creating a healthy, loving environment for your children, even it if that means you need to end your relationship.

SELF-GUIDED INTERVENTION: PRIORITISING A HEALTHY ENVIRONMENT FOR CHILDREN OVER STAYING TOGETHER

OBJECTIVE

To guide you, if you are a parent, in evaluating whether staying in your relationship 'for the kids' is truly beneficial or if separation would create a healthier, more supportive environment.

INTRODUCTION

There is a common belief that staying together for the sake of the children is the best course of action, but research shows that this is not always the case. Children are more affected by the emotional environment they grow up in than by whether their parents are together or apart. Toxic or unhappy relationships can cause anxiety, depression and behavioural issues in children, and they learn relationship dynamics from what they observe at home. As such, it's crucial for parents to model healthy relationship behaviours, whether they stay together or decide to co-parent separately. This intervention will help you understand the impact of relationship dynamics on your children's well-being and how modelling healthy behaviour, whether together or apart, is crucial for raising emotionally healthy children. The steps will help you to evaluate your relationship and make decisions that prioritise both your and your children's well-being.

PART I: UNDERSTANDING THE IMPACT OF RELATIONSHIP DYNAMICS ON CHILDREN

I. THE EMOTIONAL ENVIRONMENT MATTERS MORE THAN STAYING TOGETHER

- Children thrive in environments that are healthy and supportive. Whether parents are together or apart, what matters most is the quality of the emotional environment. Constant conflict, tension or unhappiness in the home can lead to anxiety, depression and behavioural problems in children.

- Example: 'My partner and I argued a lot, and I started noticing that our child seemed more withdrawn and anxious at school. This made me realise that staying together wasn't necessarily providing the stability we thought.'

2. MODEL HEALTHY RELATIONSHIP DYNAMICS

- Children learn by observing their parents' behaviours. If they grow up witnessing conflict, disrespect or emotional disconnection, they might internalise those patterns as normal. Conversely, when parents model healthy communication, respect and self-care, children are more likely to develop positive relationship skills.
- Example: 'We realised that by constantly arguing in front of our kids, we were teaching them that this was a normal way to interact. We decided it was time to either work on the relationship or separate so we could model healthier behaviours.'

3. SEPARATION CAN BE A POSITIVE DECISION

- Many parents stay together out of fear that separation will harm their children. While separation can be challenging, research shows that children are better off when they are raised in a peaceful, supportive environment — even if that means their parents live apart. Separation can reduce the emotional strain and model positive co-parenting dynamics.
- Example: 'After we separated, we noticed our children became more relaxed and happier, and our relationship as co-parents improved. We were finally able to focus on what was best for them.'

PART 2: EVALUATING YOUR RELATIONSHIP FOR YOUR CHILDREN'S WELL-BEING

I. ASSESS THE LEVEL OF CONFLICT IN YOUR RELATIONSHIP

- Take a step back and evaluate the level of conflict in your relationship. Are arguments frequent? Is there ongoing tension or emotional disconnect? Assessing the emotional climate of your relationship helps you understand its impact on your children.
- Example: 'We realised we were bickering daily, and that our kids were often caught in the middle. This prompted us to take a closer look at whether staying together was truly in their best interest.'

2. CONSIDER THE LONG-TERM EFFECTS OF CONFLICT

- While short-term conflict is common in any relationship, constant tension and unresolved issues can have lasting effects on children. Reflect on whether the environment at home is conducive to their emotional growth and well-being.
- Example: 'I didn't want our kids to grow up thinking that constant arguing was normal, so we started exploring other options like therapy and, eventually, separation.'

3. IDENTIFY THE POTENTIAL FOR GROWTH OR CHANGE

- Sometimes relationships can improve through counselling or changes in communication. Other times, the damage is too deep to repair. Assess whether your relationship has the potential to grow into a healthier dynamic or if separation would provide a better emotional environment for everyone involved.
- Example: 'We tried couples therapy, and while it helped, we realised we were still unhappy together. It became clear that separating was the best decision for us and for our kids.'

PART 3: CREATING A HEALTHY ENVIRONMENT FOR CHILDREN, TOGETHER OR APART

I. FOCUS ON CO-PARENTING

- If you decide to separate, prioritise co-parenting in a way that models respect, cooperation and clear communication. Children benefit from seeing their parents work together for their well-being, even if they no longer live in the same household.
- Example: 'We make it a point to have regular co-parenting check-ins, where we discuss the kids' needs and how we can provide consistency for them, even though we're no longer a couple.'

2. SET CLEAR BOUNDARIES FOR CONFLICT

- Whether you stay together or separate, it's important to set boundaries around conflict. Avoid arguing in front of your children or using them as go-betweens in disputes. Shielding them from toxic interactions helps maintain a more positive emotional environment.
- Example: 'We agreed that no matter how frustrated we were with each other, we wouldn't argue in front of the kids. Instead, we take a step back and address our issues privately.'

3. MAINTAIN OPEN COMMUNICATION WITH YOUR CHILDREN

- Children need to feel secure and informed, especially during times of transition like separation. Be open with them about what is happening, while reassuring them that they are loved and supported by both parents.
- Example: 'When we decided to separate, we sat down with our children and explained what was happening in an age-appropriate way. We made sure they knew that we both loved them and would still be there for them, even though we weren't living together any more.'

PART 4: PRIORITISING YOUR WELL-BEING AS A PARENT

I. YOUR HAPPINESS IMPACTS YOUR CHILDREN

- Your emotional health has a direct impact on your children. When parents are happier and less stressed, they are more present and engaged with their children. Taking care of your own well-being is a crucial part of being a good parent.
- Example: 'After the separation, I focused on my own mental health and well-being. I noticed that as I became happier, I was able to be more patient and attentive with my kids.'

2. SEEK SUPPORT IF NEEDED

- Separation or divorce can be a difficult transition, both emotionally and practically. Seek support from friends, family or a therapist to help you navigate this challenging time and maintain your well-being.
- Example: 'I joined a support group for single parents, which helped me cope with the emotional challenges of separating and gave me tools to better support my children.'

3. EMPHASISE SELF-CARE

- Regular self-care is essential to your well-being as a parent. Whether it's taking time for exercise, relaxation or hobbies, ensure you're taking care of yourself so you can be the best parent possible.
- Example: 'I started setting aside time each week for self-care, whether it was going for a walk or just taking a long bath. It helped me to recharge and be more present with my kids.'

CONCLUSION

Staying together for the kids may seem like the right thing to do, but a toxic or unhappy relationship can cause more harm to children than separation. Creating a healthy emotional environment, whether together or apart, is what truly matters. By focusing on your own well-being and modelling positive relationship dynamics, you can provide your children with the stability and support they need to thrive.

TAKEAWAY

It's not staying together that benefits children most — it's providing a healthy, supportive environment. Whether you stay together or separate, prioritise the modelling of respectful, caring relationship behaviours and focus on your own well-being. This will help you to create a positive space for your children's emotional growth and happiness.

'HAVING EXTERNAL
FRIENDSHIPS AND NOT
ACTING ON AN UNDERLYING
ATTRACTION IS A MEANS
OF DEMONSTRATING TRUST
AND COMMITMENT TO YOUR
RELATIONSHIP'

MYTH 15

IT'S IMPOSSIBLE TO BE CLOSE FRIENDS WITH SOMEONE WHO HAS THE POTENTIAL TO BE A ROMANTIC PARTNER

Provocative Truth: Close friendships with others can increase your attraction to and appreciation of your partner

This myth, which is closely aligned with the myth that you should never be attracted to anyone other than your partner, really fascinates me and is one that I soft survey by constantly talking about it to people and asking their opinion. What I hear the majority of the time is that if you are in a committed relationship, you shouldn't have close friends who have the potential to become romantic partners. In fact, there are still a lot of people who don't believe that men and women can be just friends.

In a recent interview, Dr Karen Gurney told me about the Kinsey Scale, which is used to measure a person's sexual orientation and shows that the majority of people are fluid, even if they don't realise it. This means that the sex of the friend is less important than if it is someone with whom a romantic attraction would be possible. However, I most often hear this myth expressed in the heteronormative terms that you shouldn't be close friends with someone of the opposite sex if you are in a serious relationship. And if there's even a hint of you being attracted to that person, you definitely shouldn't be friends with them, as that is crossing a line. In fact, for a lot of people, simply being attracted to someone else counts as an act of infidelity (as I discussed in Chapter 9). Let's say you are attracted to one of your co-workers but you're in a committed relationship. Many people would say that the line of infidelity is being crossed every moment that you talk to that person.

Underlying this myth is the implication that a close friendship is going to lead to an emotional or physical infidelity. That it's going to lead to your partner being jealous. And, ultimately, that it's going to lead to the deterioration and potential break-up of your relationship.

TRUST ISSUES

Once again, this myth is perpetuated by the media, and it is a narrative that is returned to again and again in fiction and drama. It even came up in another episode of *Young Sheldon* that I was watching with my kids. Sheldon's grandmother Meemaw was in an accident so had to take what they referred to as the 'senior citizen bus'. There was a husband and wife sitting behind her, and the husband asked Meemaw where she was going. When she replied by saying, 'I'm going to get my hair done,' the wife intervened and told her husband to stop flirting. It was obviously a joke in the context of the show, but it's a subtle indication of how ingrained this concept is in our culture. You shouldn't even be speaking to someone else in the presence of your partner.

There's also a socialisation aspect too. When we come together at a party, for example, what you normally see is that the men go off one way and the women go off another, and there is this unwritten rule that you shouldn't interact with the other side unless you're with your partner. And if you're not with your partner, you should only be talking with someone for a certain amount of time, because you don't want to cross that line. This may come down in part to evolutionary psychology: because our ancestors felt threatened by the presence of mating rivals, we have evolved to be wary of others who could potentially come between us and our partners.

It is also worth acknowledging that as a society we have a lot of insecurities and trust issues. We know that approximately half the population have avoidant, anxious or disorganised attachment styles, so they'll be even more prone to allowing insecurities and past experiences to fuel their jealousy when it comes to their partners forming a close bond with someone other than themselves. This links quite nicely to Chapter 13, because if you've got low personal well-being, you're more likely to be insecure, and that's going to increase the chances that you are jealous. If you're more secure in your attachments and you've done the work on yourself, then you're not going to worry so much about your partner having a close emotional friendship with someone else.

I think Jill must be one of the most secure people in the world. My job is to talk about relationships, and my audience is predominantly made up of women, so whenever we go to a party together, I'm inevitably surrounded by nothing but single women wanting to talk to me about my work. If Jill was insecure, she'd probably stand right next to me for the entire evening. But what actually happens is she goes off on her own as soon as we arrive and mingles, leaving me to talk and answer people's questions. We often end up being separated for hours, and I'm usually the one trying to find and hold on to her. So, it's really about how secure you feel as an individual that dictates your comfort level with your partner interacting with eligible people.

This myth also links back to the idea that you need to fulfil all of your partner's needs, and you shouldn't therefore have to go outside of your partnership for the emotional support you get from a close friendship. In fact, we have come to believe that you can't step outside of your relationship for any of the many things that you need and, if you do, that somehow means your partnership is lacking. This is especially true when it comes to close friendships with other people.

BEING ATTRACTED TO OTHER PEOPLE IS NORMAL

A University of Wisconsin study that looked at friendship found that 62 per cent of men and 45 per cent of women reported romantic attraction to their opposite-sex friends.[1] The study further revealed that such feelings of attraction often caused tension and uncertainty within their relationships. This would seem to support the belief that opposite-sex friendships can be complicated by romantic feelings and are a threat to the romantic relationship you have. However, my interpretation of this is that it reveals a conversation we don't like to have that we should be having. As we explored in Chapter 9, we have to normalise the fact that being attracted to people is a part of being human. Instead, we've normalised that it's bad to be attracted to a friend, that you shouldn't feel that way, that there's something wrong with you if do, that there's something lacking in your relationship. This then leads you down a terrible path of feeling like you can't trust yourself, or that there are issues in your relationship. It can also resurface insecurities from your past. And because you can't talk about it, you've reduced the ability to work through it and grow. As a result, your relationship satisfaction is ultimately much lower.

The main point is that feeling attracted to a friend does happen. In fact, it's common and, because of that, it's important to be able to talk about it. There should be open communication between you and your partner about this topic (although I discuss in Chapter 17 that sometimes you can divulge too much information, so a balance needs to be struck).

If you do have that discussion and are open about the fact that you have a close bond with a friend, it can actually be beneficial to your relationship. It can, for example, enhance trust and security within your relationship because the close friendship demonstrates your ability to form a bond with someone and it not lead to cheating. Additionally, when you have exposure to different perspectives through friendships, it can enhance your communication skills and increase your ability to empathise with others. It can also contribute to personal growth, because you have a broader social network. And if you have a wide social network, and your partner has a different social network, then you're bringing that crossed network effect back home and getting the benefits from that. Finally, close friendships outside of the relationship show you that your partner doesn't have to strive to meet all of your needs, thereby removing some of the unnecessary pressure that we place on our relationships. All of this ultimately increases your relationship satisfaction.

Having close emotional bonds with others can also provide a platonic perspective on gender dynamics and relationship issues. It's almost like you can extract knowledge and information and see what other people are doing. This is one way to increase your empathy and gain a better understanding of how relationships work. I have several close friends who are women, partly because the field I work in is made up predominantly of women. And because I am in the relationship space, I obviously talk a lot about relationships. But I'm not just uploading all the time; I'm listening and downloading new information too. The same goes for my female friends who are therapists and experts in my category. In this way, I learn a tonne through my friendship base of predominantly women.

This has been beneficial in my relationship with Jill, but also in my life overall. All of the skills that can be developed if we form close bonds with people outside of our relationships — ability to trust, better communication, increased empathy — we can take into every aspect of our lives.

I should admit, though, that I grew up believing this myth to be true. I always thought that you should never be close friends with people who you could have romantic feelings for or be attracted to. I even remember thinking that Jill shouldn't have any male friends, and I shouldn't have any female friends. I think it was probably developing relationships with women and seeing that this didn't mean I was going to cheat as a result — in fact, the idea that I would was actually a bit silly — that made me realise the idea you can't have close friendships with people who could be romantic interests was, in fact, a myth. I also saw that Jill had a close circle of friends, many of them men, from growing up that was beneficial for her in the same way that me having close connections with others was beneficial for me.

PUTTING TRUST INTO PRACTICE

Having close friends is a way of putting trust into practice. Jealousy and insecurity are often about the idea of something that might happen, the thought of a betrayal, but having external friendships and not acting on an underlying attraction is a means of demonstrating trust and commitment to your relationship. Again, it's similar to conflict — you have to test it out in order to be able to grow and strengthen your relationship. For example, if a very insular couple never do anything with other people, that will just exacerbate their jealousy and insecurity, potentially leading to an unhealthy codependence.

You've probably heard of helicopter parents, but there are also helicopter partners, who hover around and defend their partners from people they consider to be a threat. How people act at parties is again instructive in this regard, as it is very telling how a couple operates in a group setting. I don't think most of us are aware of what we're signalling in such a scenario. What often happens is one person tries to control their partner, prompting them as to what they should be doing — 'You said you were only going to have one drink' — and guarding them from unwelcome attention. This sort of behaviour screams that there are trust and insecurity issues. Another such signal that I see all the time is when one person is having a laugh with someone else and their partner puts their arm around them, as if to say, 'Just so you know, I'm right here.'

With stronger couples, it's the opposite. You'll see one partner go and grab someone and bring them over to talk to their partner if they think they will hit it off or have something in common. If you're more of a helicopter partner, it's important to access your feelings and emotions in these moments, and then to begin to label them and understand what they are and why they're coming up so you know what your triggers are.

♥

Ultimately, close friendships outside of the relationship, even with people who could potentially be romantic partners, are going to be to the benefit of your relationship, as they foster trust and make you both more confident, well-rounded individuals.

SELF-GUIDED INTERVENTION: CHALLENGING THE MYTH OF OPPOSITE-SEX FRIENDSHIPS THREATENING RELATIONSHIPS*

OBJECTIVE

To help you understand that opposite-sex friendships can enhance, rather than threaten, romantic relationships.

INTRODUCTION

There is a common belief that close opposite-sex friendships pose a threat to romantic relationships, with many people viewing them as a pathway to emotional or physical infidelity. However, research and personal experience show that such friendships can increase trust, empathy and appreciation for your partner. Opposite-sex friendships provide a fresh perspective on relationship dynamics and help partners to grow emotionally, all while reinforcing the bond of the romantic relationship. This intervention aims to foster trust, reduce jealousy and improve emotional regulation, ultimately strengthening your relationship dynamics by normalising and supporting healthy platonic friendships. The steps will guide you in overcoming insecurities while fostering trust and open communication.

PART I: UNDERSTANDING THE ROLE OF OPPOSITE-SEX FRIENDSHIPS

I. OPPOSITE-SEX FRIENDSHIPS PROVIDE NEW PERSPECTIVES

- Friendships with people of the opposite sex can offer insights into different gender dynamics, providing a deeper understanding of relationship issues and helping you develop empathy.

---

* Although the intervention focuses on opposite-sex friendships, it also applies to close outside friendships in same-sex relationships.

These friendships broaden your social network, allowing you to bring new knowledge and experiences back into your romantic relationship.

- Example: 'Having a close female friend has helped me better understand certain emotional cues and communication styles that I hadn't fully appreciated before, which has strengthened my relationship with my partner.'

2. ATTRACTION TO FRIENDS IS NORMAL AND MANAGEABLE

- Studies show that attraction to friends is not uncommon. However, it's important to understand that attraction doesn't automatically lead to infidelity. Open conversations about attraction and platonic boundaries can foster trust and reduce jealousy.
- Example: 'I've occasionally felt attracted to a friend, but talking openly with my partner about these feelings has actually made us closer, as we trust each other to maintain healthy boundaries.'

3. TRUST IS BUILT THROUGH BOUNDARIES AND COMMUNICATION

- Trust isn't about avoiding potential challenges; it's about navigating them with openness and honesty. Building trust requires communication about feelings, clear boundaries and an understanding that opposite-sex friendships can enrich your relationship.
- Example: 'When my partner and I discussed our close friendships, we set boundaries that made us both feel comfortable. It's brought us closer because we trust each other to maintain those boundaries.'

PART 2: ADDRESSING INSECURITIES AND JEALOUSY

I. IDENTIFY AND ACKNOWLEDGE JEALOUSY

- The first step in managing jealousy is acknowledging when it occurs. Recognise that jealousy often stems from personal insecurities or past experiences, not necessarily from the actions of your partner.
- Example: 'When I noticed feeling jealous of my partner's new friendship, I paused and asked myself why. I realised it wasn't about their relationship but rather my own insecurity about not spending enough quality time together.'

2. USE COGNITIVE REAPPRAISAL TO REFRAME JEALOUS THOUGHTS

- Cognitive reappraisal is a technique to challenge negative emotions and replace them with more constructive thoughts. Identify your feelings, challenge the thoughts driving them and reframe them with positive evidence (see below for more on this).
- Example: 'I felt jealous when my partner spent time with their friend, but I reminded myself that my partner has always been trustworthy and this friendship is not a threat. They've always been open about it, and I have no reason to doubt them.'

3. PRACTISE OPEN COMMUNICATION

- When feelings of jealousy arise, communicate them openly with your partner in a non-confrontational way. Discuss your feelings, listen to your partner's perspective and work together to establish boundaries that support both of you.
- Example: 'I shared with my partner that I was feeling uneasy about their friendship with a co-worker. We had a calm conversation about it, and I learned that they value my trust and are committed to keeping clear boundaries.'

PART 3: STRENGTHENING YOUR RELATIONSHIP
THROUGH PLATONIC FRIENDSHIPS

I. RECOGNISE THE BENEFITS OF EXTERNAL FRIENDSHIPS

- Having close friendships outside your romantic relationship can reduce the pressure on your partner to fulfil all of your emotional needs. This not only strengthens your bond but also brings new energy and perspectives into your relationship.
- Example: 'Since developing close friendships outside of our relationship, I've noticed we rely less on each other for every little emotional need, and it's allowed us both to grow as individuals.'

2. ENCOURAGE SOCIAL NETWORKS OUTSIDE OF THE RELATIONSHIP

- Healthy relationships allow space for both of you to have friendships and social networks outside of your relationship. This fosters independence, reduces codependence and strengthens the relationship dynamic.
- Example: 'My partner has their own set of friends, and I have mine. It's made our relationship more interesting because we're always learning new things and sharing experiences with one another.'

3. BUILD TRUST BY RESPECTING BOUNDARIES

- Trust is built over time by respecting the boundaries you and your partner have agreed upon. If either of you feels uncomfortable about a friendship, revisit the boundaries together and adjust them as needed to maintain trust and comfort.
- Example: 'We regularly check in with one another to make sure our friendships and boundaries still feel comfortable. This ongoing communication keeps jealousy at bay and builds trust.'

PART 4: PUTTING TRUST INTO PRACTICE WITH OPPOSITE-SEX FRIENDSHIPS

I. TEST TRUST IN SMALL SITUATIONS

- Trust doesn't just exist — it's something that needs to be practised and tested in everyday situations. Encourage your partner's friendships and notice how trust strengthens when it is honoured over time.
- Example: 'When my partner went out with their friend, I focused on trusting them. Over time, I saw that their friendship didn't diminish our bond, and it built my confidence in our relationship.'

2. AVOID HELICOPTER PARTNERING

- Hovering around your partner, especially in social settings, can signal insecurity and mistrust. Practise giving your partner space in social situations and trust that their interactions won't harm your relationship.
- Example: 'At social events, I make a point to let my partner mingle without me hovering. It's a way to show them — and myself — that I trust them completely.'

3. REFLECT ON YOUR OWN FRIENDSHIPS

- Take time to evaluate your own friendships, particularly with people of the opposite sex. How do they contribute to your personal growth? How do they impact your romantic relationship? This reflection can help you appreciate the value of these connections.
- Example: 'I reflected on my own friendships and realised how much I've learned from my female friends. It's enriched my relationship by giving me new perspectives and improving my communication skills.'

CONCLUSION

Opposite-sex friendships don't have to be a threat to your romantic relationship. In fact, when handled with trust, communication and boundaries, these friendships can enhance your relationship, providing new perspectives and reducing the pressure on your partner to meet all your emotional needs. Trust, emotional security and open communication are the foundation for maintaining both romantic relationships and healthy friendships.

THE INTERVENTION IN PRACTICE

One technique that I use in my own life that can be effective when it comes to challenging this myth is called cognitive reappraisal, which is essentially just a means of reducing negative emotions, enhancing positive emotions and promoting problem-solving. The idea is that, whenever you feel off, you first identify what the emotion is; for example, if you feel anxious or angry or sad. The second step is to identify the thought and work out what is driving the emotion: *I'm going to fail at this presentation* or *My partner doesn't care about me*. Third, you challenge the thought by looking for counterevidence. And the fourth step is reframing your initial reaction.

I'll give you an example of cognitive reappraisal that relates to my work. I was recently offered the opportunity to get involved in a new project, but before I could commit to it, I had to run it by another work partner. I sent all of the relevant information about the new project to my point of contact, but when I woke up the next morning, I hadn't received a response. I started to go through the process of understanding my reaction and how I felt: *I'm angry. I feel disrespected.* Then I moved on to identifying the thought, which was, *Oh my gosh, they're going to try to prevent me from doing this new project.* I found my thoughts running off to the extreme: *They're going to try to kill my career.* This is where the all-important third step comes in: challenge the thought and ask yourself how valid it is. Is what you're thinking based on facts or assumptions? What's the evidence to support or contradict this thought? In this scenario, I said to myself, *They did say a few months ago that I could do it, and they have already introduced me to the publicist to talk about the announcement of the new project, so they probably aren't trying to block it.* I also realised that it was a holiday weekend, and I'd sent over the details quite late on the Friday, so it was likely just a case of my contact being busy or not having seen my request yet, rather than them being disrespectful. In this way, I was able to do step four and recalibrate my gut reaction to land at a more reasonable position: *It's not the end of the world if it gets resolved next week.*

The benefits of going through this process are that it gives you immediate emotional relief and leads to more stable and positive emotional health in the long term. It also helps you with your emotional regulation and boosts your resilience, because it gives you a more constructive outlook that allows you to better deal with any challenges that come up. And you can apply this technique to any aspect of your relationship or life. I know that it's helped me to see things differently on numerous occasions.

TAKEAWAY

Normalise opposite-sex friendships as part of a healthy relationship dynamic. Practise trust, set clear boundaries and use cognitive reappraisal to manage feelings of jealousy. By embracing platonic friendships and nurturing open communication, you can strengthen your romantic relationship and create a deeper bond with your partner.

'THE ODDS ARE THAT YOU WILL BE ABLE TO OVERCOME INFIDELITY SUCCESSFULLY, AND THE UPSIDE IS THAT YOU COULD EVEN HAVE HIGHER SATISFACTION THAN YOU HAD BEFORE'

MYTH 16

INFIDELITY MEANS THE END OF A RELATIONSHIP

Provocative Truth: By focusing on forgiveness and
rebuilding trust, many relationships can recover
from infidelity and become stronger

'Once a cheater always a cheater' has been repeated so often that I think most people today believe that infidelity inevitably means the end of a relationship. But the provocative truth is that it doesn't have to, and couples who effectively work through infidelity can strengthen their relationships and not only stay together, but even come out the other side with higher satisfaction.

The benefits of trying to overcome infidelity in your relationship include, first and foremost, a stronger relationship in the long run. When I interviewed the Gottmans for my podcast, they told me that more than two-thirds of couples who go through their programme after experiencing infidelity come out stronger and with renewed relationship satisfaction. So, the odds are that you will be able to overcome infidelity successfully, and the upside is that you could even have higher satisfaction than you had before.

However, the sad reality is, the vast majority of couples who experience infidelity, whether emotional or physical, will either break up or have low satisfaction for the rest of their relationship.[1] Perhaps that's not particularly surprising when you consider that

Eli Finkel's research has revealed that most couples today have low satisfaction anyway. So, if you don't have the right relationship skills and you have chosen or been selected by the wrong partner, and then you throw infidelity into that mix, it's a terrible combination. But it doesn't necessarily have to be that way.

WHY IS THERE ZERO TOLERANCE OF INFIDELITY?

One of the main reasons why people believe this myth to be true is, of course, the cultural narratives around infidelity. We are constantly being told, whether via television, film, novels or pop music, that if someone cheats on you, that's the end. There is also a false narrative that it takes a lifetime to build trust but a moment to lose it, and once it's lost, it's gone forever. In other words, when trust is broken, it can never be repaired. But that's just not the case. Trust is not a fixed quality, and it can be repaired, although it admittedly takes longer to build trust back up than it does to undermine it.

The bottom line is that there is zero tolerance when it comes to infidelity in Western culture, but, historically speaking, this has been true for women for a lot longer than it has been for men. In fact, it again dates to the creation of the nuclear family. I recently visited Stratford-upon-Avon, where I learned that William Shakespeare's daughter was tried for adultery. She successfully defended herself, but a man would never have been put on trial for an infidelity.

This inequality began to be challenged with the rise of feminism in the late 1960s and early 1970s, and today there is total condemnation when it comes to infidelity, with society critical of any sort of cheating, whether in a heteronormative, same-sex or any other sort of relationship. But what constitutes cheating in any given relationship is subjective. You could be in a polyamorous relationship, and committing an infidelity outside the agreed boundaries is just as much of a betrayal as it would be if there were only two partners in the relationship. Infidelity is therefore how you define it within your relationship, which is why this needs to be established from the outset. Also, studies show that emotional infidelity elicits more anxiety and jealousy than sexual infidelity, and so for many it will be harder to recover from.[2] This further emphasises the need for discussions about what infidelity means to you when you embark on a long-term relationship, just as early discussions about physical and emotional attraction are necessary (as discussed in Chapter 9).

Even if there is infidelity according to the agreed terms, I strongly believe that too many relationships end prematurely and therefore miss an opportunity for growth. Immediately hitting the eject button if there is infidelity perpetuates the stigma around it, and you'll have developed no skills — for example, learning how to forgive or receive someone else's forgiveness, or understanding how trust can be rebuilt. Then, when you embark on another relationship, you are more likely to get out as soon as there is any hint of an infraction. So, in a way, you're putting yourself at a disadvantage if you leave without even attempting to reconcile.

TOP REASONS FOR INFIDELITY

The research shows that couples who experience infidelity typically report very low pre-existing levels of satisfaction, and their relationships are characterised by poor communication, lack of emotional intimacy, unmet needs and so on.[3] More specifically, the consensus seems to be that the main reasons infidelity is committed are emotional dissatisfaction, with one or both people feeling neglected by the other so they seek support and connection from someone else, and sexual dissatisfaction. Opportunity and risk-taking behaviour are also large contributors. In other words, having the opportunity to cheat, combined with a tendency towards risk-taking behaviour, increases the likelihood that infidelity will occur. It is easy to dismiss someone like that as just being a cheat, but if your partner is impulsive by nature, limiting their opportunity to act on that impulsivity is sensible. To do this and reduce the risk of infidelity, it's crucial to create a relationship environment that promotes transparency and mutual accountability. Engaging in open conversations about boundaries and building a structure of trust helps. Additionally, encouraging your partner to be mindful of situations that might trigger impulsive behaviour and working together to avoid risky scenarios can be effective strategies. That said, personal responsibility is still important.

Another contributing factor to infidelity is how we saw love play out in our own families. If an impulsive person with an insecure attachment style saw both their parents commit infidelity, and they're at a party on their own, well, that's a bad recipe, and opportunity meeting risk-taking behaviour is more likely to play itself out negatively.

Another reason for infidelity is lack of commitment to the relationship. And the last one that I'll underscore, because the list goes on and on, is a person's own unresolved personal issues leading to them cheating. So, their low self-esteem, their insecurities, their unresolved trauma, their desire to seek validation all play into the mix. As such, it is often not a problem with the relationship that causes the infidelity to occur so much as an individual's own personal issues.

When it comes to the strongest traits that are indicative of someone who might commit an act of infidelity, impulsivity is number one. So, if your partner has no discipline around any sort of temptation, that's a strong sign. But you also have to watch out for narcissists and people who lack empathy, as they just don't care about your feelings and are liable to cheat as well.

Impulsivity, narcissism and lack of empathy: if you're witnessing those traits in your partner, that's a bad cocktail. This goes back to why the selection of your partner is so critical (as I discussed in *Find Love*), because if you're in a relationship with an impulsive narcissist who has no empathy for you, then you're in for a world of hurt. You'll likely be walking on eggshells all the time, because you're going to be fearful of what will happen next.

It's best to avoid someone who scores high in those types of traits in the first place, but if your partner exhibits some of these characteristics at the lower end of the spectrum, then you'll hopefully be able to mitigate some of the risk if you've done some of the work that we're talking about in this book. If you're with someone who is not necessarily a full-blown narcissist but can be quite impulsive from time to time, and you build up trust, apologise frequently, communicate and know how to overcome conflict in your relationship, then that will also help to mitigate the chances that a person will act on their impulsivity. However, infidelity sometimes happens regardless.

HOW COMMON IS CHEATING?

I was on a show a few years ago and the host wanted me to give her a percentage for the number of relationships in which infidelity occurs. At the time, I knew it to be about a third; however, the host pushed back and said something along the lines of, 'I don't buy that. That's not my experience, and that's not my friends' experience. Also, I don't trust the data, because I'm sure lots of people who have cheated just lie when they are asked. It must be much higher than that!'

I wish I'd had the knowledge then to give her a better answer, but I went away and tried to understand how infidelity studies are done. And, yes, a lot of the data is self-reported, but there are a variety of ways in which researchers check the accuracy of people's responses. Then you have behavioural reports from therapists who work with couples to help inform the numbers, and you can also look at the direct behaviour of couples, such as their patterns of communication, and their emotional responses and interactions, to assess relational health and the potential for infidelity. That's where the approximately 30 per cent figure comes from. Then, within that group, a similar number, in the region of 20–30 per cent, are repeat offenders. This is a smaller percentage of people who are committing acts of emotional and physical infidelity than I think most people would imagine — just like the host on that show, I think the majority of people would guess it is more like 50 per cent or even more. Now, one act of infidelity is too many, but it's worth underscoring that cheating is still the exception, not the rule.

It is also worth pointing out that there is a difference between how men and women typically respond to emotional and physical infidelity. Most men report that it doesn't really bother them if their partner is emotionally intimate — with someone at work, for example — whereas for women it's the opposite.[4] From a male perspective, an emotional infidelity could be serious or significant, but you can also see how there is a whole list of other things that could be considered more disruptive. Now, if it was physical, it would be different, as most men report that they would have a real problem in that scenario. However, emotional infidelity is still cheating, and the reaction to it is subjective.

Some people might argue that infidelity is the biggest challenge you could ever face as a couple and if you can overcome it, then you can overcome anything, but I would argue that, yes, it's hard, but there are other things in life, such as the loss of loved ones and serious illness, that are much more difficult to navigate as a couple. Although cheating is a significant source of conflict within relationships, the fact that it is not necessarily the most difficult to overcome is supported by the number of couples who are able to get past it.

ADVICE FOR COUPLES WHO EXPERIENCE INFIDELITY IN THEIR RELATIONSHIPS

It all begins and ends with forgiveness. One study reports that couples who engage in forgiveness report higher satisfaction levels, and 25 per cent of them even reach higher levels of satisfaction over time than previously.[5] So, it boils down to: can the wronged party bring themselves to forgive their partner, and can their partner accept their forgiveness so that both can move on together?

How the infidelity was discovered plays a big part in the outcome. When you find out a partner is cheating without them disclosing it to you, there is a much lower likelihood that you're going to be able to reconcile and save the relationship. But if you've got a partner who's come to you and has admitted to the act of infidelity, there's a higher likelihood that you'll be able to repair it. So, the guilty party being remorseful and willing to own their mistake is key. Do they have awareness and understand their role in what has happened? Do they appreciate the impact that it's had on you and your emotional well-being?

There is an exercise that I use frequently on *Married at First Sight* that seems incredibly simple at first glance but proves to be quite challenging for most people: after listening to your partner express how they feel, you must name the emotions behind their words. This exercise is particularly helpful in navigating infidelity because it promotes empathy and emotional understanding, which are critical in rebuilding trust. Many people, particularly men, find it difficult to articulate emotions due to social conditioning, making it harder to connect those words with what they're truly experiencing. In cases of infidelity, emotional disconnection is often at the root, so this exercise is vital in repairing that disconnect.

The key here is distinguishing between emotions and feelings. Emotions are our automatic responses, while feelings are the
learned, psychological reactions to those emotions. When infidelity occurs, each partner may experience the same emotions, like
anger or fear, but their feelings and behaviours in response to
those emotions may differ. This exercise helps you understand not
just your partner's emotions, but also the unique way they process
and react to them, which is essential for developing empathy. By
naming and recognising these emotions, you create a space where
both of you feel seen and understood — an essential first step in
healing from betrayal and reconnecting.

We shoot *Married at First Sight* over two months and, in that
time, people want to see couples who have gone through infidelity
and come out the other side in a place of bliss. But it actually takes
two to five years on average for a couple to get past an infidelity, so it is not a quick process. I feel that's important to emphasise. You can't just see a therapist and expect things to be back to
normal overnight. It might take seeing multiple therapists, and it
will require you to do work as a couple and as an individual. The
work required is what I've been talking about in this book: it's
the check-ins, the apologising, the understanding how to resolve
conflict and so on. When a big test such as infidelity comes along,
you have to draw on all of your skills. You can't just deploy the fact
that you're empathetic or a good listener. The individual Avengers
couldn't defeat Thanos on their own — it took all of them. I know
that doesn't give a nice, neat answer, but dealing with infidelity
really does require you to deploy everything.

That's why it's such a good opportunity for growth, personally
and within the relationship, because you have to bring all of your
skills to bear. If you just break up as soon as the infidelity is discovered and don't at least try to work through the issue, even if you
are ultimately unsuccessful, you're not going to develop the skills
to the same extent to help you thrive moving forward.

SELF-GUIDED INTERVENTION: HEALING FROM INFIDELITY – A PATH TO FORGIVENESS AND REBUILDING TRUST

OBJECTIVE

To guide you through the process of healing after infidelity.

INTRODUCTION

One of the highlights of my career was interviewing Drs Julie and John Gottman for my *We Need to Talk* podcast, where we discussed their remarkable methodology for healing from infidelity. Their 'Atone, Attune, Attach' method offers one of the most effective paths for overcoming betrayal, with 70 per cent of couples coming out stronger.[6] I highly recommend their programme for those going through this difficult journey. However, in the interim, this intervention, based on their approach, can help you to take the first steps towards healing and rebuilding your relationship.

PART I: ATONING FOR THE INFIDELITY

I. ACKNOWLEDGE THE BETRAYAL

- The partner who has committed the infidelity must take full responsibility for their actions without minimising or excusing their behaviour. Atonement begins with owning the mistake and acknowledging the pain caused.
- Example: 'I know I hurt you deeply by betraying your trust, and I am truly sorry for the pain I've caused. I take full responsibility for my actions.'

2. SINCERELY APOLOGISE AND SHOW REMORSE

- Apologising sincerely is critical to starting the healing process. The apology must express genuine remorse, show understanding of the hurt inflicted and commit to being transparent moving forward. The wronged partner must feel that the apology is heartfelt and not just words.

- Example: 'I deeply regret my actions and how they've affected our relationship. I understand that I've broken your trust, and I'm committed to doing whatever it takes to repair the damage.'

3. BE TRANSPARENT AND ACCOUNTABLE

- Transparency is key in rebuilding trust. This involves being open about your actions, answering any questions your partner may have and being completely transparent in your communication and whereabouts moving forward.
- Example: 'I'm going to be completely transparent about my schedule, who I'm with and what I'm doing. I want you to feel safe and secure in our relationship again.'

4. SEEK THERAPY IF NEEDED

- It may be helpful for both of you to seek individual or couples therapy during the atonement phase. Therapy can offer a safe space to discuss feelings and begin the healing process.
- Example: 'I think it would be helpful for us to talk to a therapist together so we can work through this in a way that strengthens our relationship.'

PART 2: ATTUNING TO EACH OTHER'S EMOTIONS

I. LISTEN AND EMPATHISE

- The attuning step involves becoming emotionally connected and empathetic to your partner's feelings. The partner who was wronged needs to be able to express their pain, anger and confusion, while the partner who committed the infidelity must listen without defensiveness.
- Example: 'I want to hear everything you're feeling. I know this is incredibly painful, and I'm here to listen, even if it's hard for me to hear.'

2. NAME THE EMOTIONS

- An exercise I often recommend is to listen to your partner's feelings and then name the emotions behind them (see above). This simple yet powerful technique helps deepen empathy and emotional understanding, especially in cases of infidelity.
- Example: After listening to your partner, say, 'It sounds like you're feeling betrayed, hurt and angry, and I completely understand why.'

3. CREATE A SAFE EMOTIONAL SPACE

- Both partners must feel safe to express their emotions. The wronged partner should feel free to express their pain without fear of judgement, and the partner who committed the infidelity must be prepared to hear it without becoming defensive.
- Example: 'I know this is painful, and I want you to feel safe expressing how you feel. I won't get defensive, and I want us to work through this together.'

4. SCHEDULE REGULAR CHECK-INS

- Healing from infidelity takes time, and regular check-ins are essential to attune emotionally on an ongoing basis. These check-ins help gauge where each of you is emotionally, ensuring that progress is being made and that both of you feel heard and understood.
- Example: 'Let's set aside time every week to check in with each other about how we're feeling. I want to make sure we're staying connected and continuing to heal.'

PART 3: REBUILDING TRUST AND ATTACHMENT

I. REBUILD TRUST GRADUALLY

- Trust is not a fixed quality — it can be rebuilt, but it takes time and effort. Rebuilding trust involves consistent, trustworthy behaviour, transparency and open communication. It's a slow process but one that can lead to a stronger relationship if done right.

- Example: 'I know it will take time for you to trust me again, but I'm committed to showing you through my actions that I'm worthy of that trust.'

2. STRENGTHEN EMOTIONAL INTIMACY

- Rebuilding trust is deeply tied to emotional intimacy. After infidelity, couples often need to work on reconnecting emotionally by being vulnerable with one another. This means sharing thoughts, fears and desires openly and creating an environment where both of you feel safe to be vulnerable.
- Example: 'I want us to feel close again, emotionally and physically. Let's work on sharing our feelings openly so we can rebuild that connection.'

3. SCHEDULE TIME FOR INTIMACY

- Physical intimacy can be difficult to rebuild after infidelity, but emotional intimacy often paves the way. While spontaneous moments of connection may feel strained, scheduling time for physical and emotional intimacy can help gradually rebuild attachment.
- Example: 'Let's set aside time each week just to be together, whether that's a date night or simply spending time reconnecting emotionally.'

4. BUILD NEW SHARED EXPERIENCES

- Shared activities help create positive memories and foster attachment. Rebuilding the relationship is not just about addressing the past, but also about creating a new future together. Engaging in new activities or revisiting old traditions can help reignite connection.

- Example: 'Let's try something new together — maybe take a cooking class or go hiking this weekend. I think doing things we enjoy together will help us reconnect.'

CONCLUSION

Infidelity does not have to mean the end of a relationship. With the right approach, couples can work through betrayal and come out stronger on the other side. The Gottmans' 'Atone, Attune, Attach' method offers a powerful framework for rebuilding trust, fostering emotional intimacy and creating a renewed attachment. While the process is difficult and requires patience, the rewards can be transformative for both of you.

THE INTERVENTION IN PRACTICE

During my own work and research, I've often drawn inspiration from the Gottmans' 'Atone, Attune, Attach' method. One particularly powerful exercise I tried with Jill involved naming the emotions behind her words during a difficult conversation. We had a rough patch where work was keeping me distant and Jill felt neglected.

One evening, she opened up about how she was feeling, and instead of just saying 'I'm sorry,' I worked on naming her emotions. I said, 'It sounds like you're feeling lonely and disconnected because I haven't been as present.' This simple act of acknowledging her emotions made a huge difference in how we communicated moving forward, and it brought us closer because she felt truly heard.

TAKEAWAY

Forgiveness, attuning emotionally and rebuilding trust are key elements of healing from infidelity. Through sincere atonement, regular check-ins and creating new shared experiences, you and your partner can come out of this challenge with a stronger bond and deeper emotional connection. Start by taking small, consistent steps and, over time, healing and trust will begin to rebuild.

'KNOWING WHEN TO
WITHHOLD CERTAIN
TRUTHS CAN STRENGTHEN
YOUR BOND'

MYTH 17

YOU SHOULD NEVER KEEP SECRETS FROM YOUR PARTNER

Provocative Truth: Balancing honesty and protection in relationships is nuanced, and sometimes withholding certain truths can be the right choice

There is a widespread belief that partners should share everything, trust one another implicitly and have no hidden aspects of their lives. This is reinforced when people say things like, 'I'm an open book,' 'We have full transparency' and 'In order to be vulnerable, you have to first be open.' All of these buzzword-y phrases suggest that you have to tell it all.

As I mentioned earlier, we all have a public life, a personal life and a secret life, and it is the sharing of our secret life that allows for the highest level of emotional intimacy. Some people might equate this with the need to be fully open with their partner, but that's not how I see it, and there's some really good research to back up my position (more of which in a bit).

FULL DISCLOSURE IS NOT ALWAYS WISE

One of the negatives of believing in this myth is a loss of personal boundaries. If you think you have to share everything, you could end up feeling as though you have lost some of your autonomy, which is a key component Carol Ryff's six dimensions of well-being that I mentioned previously on page 17. Believing in this myth will also increase unhealthy conflict, because full transparency will almost certainly lead to unnecessary disagreements over minor issues and past mistakes that hold little or no relevance to today. Next, there's an emotional burden on you when you have to share every single detail, and it can place a similar burden on your partner, who might feel overwhelmed by all the information and obliged to respond in a certain way: 'You've told me everything, now I need to do the same.' And, paradoxically, the pressure to be completely honest can actually lead to the erosion as opposed to the increase of trust if you feel as though you don't have any privacy and can't keep anything to yourself.

When it comes to personal boundaries, let's say that Sarah feels compelled to share the intimate details of her interactions with her ex-partner with her current partner, Ahmed. This includes all the trivial conversations, all the social media interactions, everything that Sarah has done with her ex-partner over time. Ahmed can start to feel insecure and begin to mistrust Sarah, even though those interactions were harmless. And Sarah can feel constantly scrutinised and as though she has no personal space or private life outside of her relationship with Ahmed, leading to an intense feeling of suffocation.

Here's an example of how telling your partner everything can lead to increased conflict. Mike says he's going to be completely transparent with his partner, Steve, and tells him about every minor annoyance that he feels towards him, complaining when Steve leaves the dishes in the sink and talks too loudly on the phone. But these issues are all minor, and bringing them up will make Steve feel constantly criticised and attacked, leading to an increase in the number of arguments and a growing sense of resentment between them.

And imagine this scenario, which illuminates how full transparency can lead to the erosion of trust. Charlie tells her partner Aanya about every single past romantic relationship that she's had . . . in detail. Casual flings, one-night stands, serious relationships, everything. She gives a full play-by-play account. But all of these events happened before they met, and they could simply lead to Aanya feeling insecure and doubting Charlie's commitment to her. In addition, the pressure for complete honesty could lead to Aanya actually feeling mistrustful and anxious about their relationship stability, even if Charlie's intentions were good.

CHOOSE WHAT TO SHARE

So, if full disclosure isn't always the best policy, what is the alternative? One study found that individuals who practise selective disclosure, where they choose to share only what's relevant and consider the potential impact on their relationship, report higher satisfaction.[1] This approach helps maintain personal boundaries while fostering trust and intimacy. The key factors to consider when deciding how much to disclose include the timing, content and emotional readiness of both partners. The study revealed that relationship satisfaction was, on average, 20 per cent higher for those who used selective disclosure compared to those who practised full transparency.

Another study found that while honesty is important, in certain types of disclosures, especially those perceived as intentionally hurtful, it can actually damage relationship quality.[2] In other words, disclosures that are too blunt or critical can lead to emotional hurt, decreased trust and increased conflict within a relationship. This study suggested that a balanced approach to honesty, whereby the potential emotional impact of any disclosure is considered, is much more beneficial for the health of a relationship. It found that partners who practised full disclosure,

leading to hurtful disclosures, albeit unintentionally, had satisfaction scores that were 30 per cent lower than those who did
not report such disclosures. Whereas couples who practised a
balanced approach to honesty had conflict frequency scores that
were 50 per cent lower than those who adhered to full transparency without any consideration for the emotional impact of what
they were disclosing.

And then, lastly, a book by Professors Sandra Petronio and
Irwin Altman discusses a theory called Communication Privacy
Management, which highlights the importance of managing
private information in relationships.[3] They found that effective
boundary coordination, whereby partners negotiate and respect
one another's privacy needs, was linked to higher relationship
satisfaction. So, establishing privacy rules ahead of time and determining what is shared and what remains private helps to maintain a healthy balance between openness and your boundaries,
which then creates trust and intimacy. Couples who use effective boundary coordination were linked to a 15 per cent increase
in relationship satisfaction scores as measured by a relationship
assessment scale.

This makes it clear that if you're using selective disclosure,
negotiating what your boundaries around privacy are, and those
boundaries are being respected, and you are being considerate as
to the emotional impact of what you are disclosing, it's a much
more effective strategy for the health of your relationship than
full disclosure.

THE DISCLOSURE CHECKLIST

When it comes to what to disclose and when, it's not just the
emotional impact that you need to take into consideration. I have
created an easy-to-understand checklist of five things to consider
before making a disclosure:

- Share what's relevant: This means information or opinions that directly affect your relationship or your partner. So, if it impacts your shared goals, your daily life or mutual decisions, it's relevant. You stay quiet if the information is trivial, out-dated or doesn't really affect your partner or your relationship today and in the future.
- Consider the emotional impact: Share information, even if it's potentially difficult, when it's necessary for the honesty of your relationship, but share it thoughtfully. And stay quiet if the truth could cause unnecessary harm or distress without any constructive outcome. In other words, you have to weigh the potential emotional impact before disclosing something. For example, say there's been an infidelity in the relationship that has already been uncovered or disclosed. Would it benefit the injured party to know that the infidelity happened in the bed-room they shared with their partner? Probably not. It would just lead to more hurt, and it wouldn't help in the couple's efforts to reconcile. I'm not, however, saying you should with-hold important details from your partner — I'm just saying you need to consider the emotional impact before you share.
- Respect boundaries: You need to ensure that what you're disclosing is building on the relationship's intimacy and trust rather than eroding it. For example, you should avoid sharing details that your partner has explicitly stated they don't want to know or that violate the personal boundaries they have previously set out.
- Choose the right moment: I talked about this in Chapter 2 when we discussed conflict resolution, but it is applicable to almost anything you want to share with your partner. It is always best to choose a time when your partner is likely to be receptive to what you have to say and is not stressed or distracted. So, avoid bringing up important or potentially upsetting topics during high-stress times, late at night or in a

public setting. This means ensuring that you both have the time and space to discuss important matters. That's not deciding five minutes before you are about to go to bed to say, 'Hey, let me tell you about this infidelity.'

- Be constructive, not hurtful: Always frame your honesty in constructive ways. Use 'I' statements (see page 34). Express your feelings. Stay quiet if you think that what you're about to say is going to come off as criticism or blame without any constructive purpose. If it is something that you still need to share, reconsider how you are going to say it.

You won't know where your partner's boundaries lie, for example, unless you've discussed it ahead of time and built up an awareness of what you both consider to be relevant or private. But if you have the discussion and put the five points of the checklist into practice, it will reduce conflict and protect your emotions, as both partners will be spared from information that might lead to undue stress or emotional pain. This will help you to preserve autonomy, and a sense of individual identity and personal space. And you can actually enhance trust, which is built on the foundation of mutual respect and understanding, not just transparency. Knowing when to withhold certain truths can strengthen your bond. This might seem to fly in the face of what most people think, but I am confident the evidence supports this point of view.

It might also seem slightly paradoxical or counter-intuitive, but, when you think about it, not needing to know everything does correlate with a greater level of trust, because sharing every single little detail ultimately suggests insecurity. Lots of people go with full transparency, perhaps because they're genuinely remorseful or they want to build the strength of their relationship, and what they've heard in pop culture is just to disclose it all so your partner knows that they can trust you. However, as we have seen, that approach can actually be damaging.

This all speaks to one of the recurring themes of the book: personal independence is really important in your relationship. It's not about subsuming your own personality within a partnership. And you can earn a more secure attachment by putting into practice my five key points and building the sort of trust that acknowledges the fact that full disclosure is not always the best way.

SELF-GUIDED INTERVENTION: USING SELECTIVE DISCLOSURE IN RELATIONSHIPS – BALANCING OPENNESS WITH PROTECTION

OBJECTIVE

To help you and your partner navigate the balance between transparency and personal boundaries, fostering trust and intimacy without overwhelming one another.

INTRODUCTION

There is a common belief that full transparency is essential in a relationship and that partners should share everything. While openness is important, research shows that full disclosure can sometimes lead to unnecessary conflict, emotional distress and a loss of personal boundaries. Selective disclosure – choosing what to share and when – helps you to maintain autonomy and emotional health while fostering trust. This intervention will guide you on how to use selective disclosure to maintain emotional well-being, respect boundaries and reduce unnecessary conflict. The steps will help you to determine what to disclose, protecting both your and your partner's well-being.

PART I: UNDERSTANDING SELECTIVE DISCLOSURE

I. SELECTIVE DISCLOSURE IMPROVES RELATIONSHIP SATISFACTION

- Full disclosure is not always wise. Research shows that practising selective disclosure — sharing relevant information based on timing, content and emotional readiness — leads to higher relationship satisfaction. By considering what's truly necessary to share, you maintain healthy personal boundaries while promoting intimacy.
- Example: 'Instead of telling my partner every single detail about my past relationships, I only share what's relevant to our current relationship. This helps avoid unnecessary jealousy or insecurity.'

2. AVOID OVERLOADING WITH UNNECESSARY DETAILS

- Sharing every minor detail from your past or present interactions can overwhelm your partner and lead to unhealthy conflict. Disclosing irrelevant information, like minor annoyances or past mistakes that have no bearing on your current relationship, can create tension and erode trust.
- Example: 'I used to complain about every little thing that bothered me, but I realised it was causing more stress than necessary. Now, I only bring up issues that really matter.'

3. BOUNDARIES STRENGTHEN TRUST

- Keeping some personal experiences or thoughts private can enhance trust by respecting boundaries. Trust is built on respect, not on knowing every detail about your partner's life. When you and your partner discuss and respect each other's privacy needs, it actually strengthens your bond.
- Example: 'We've agreed that there are certain things we won't discuss in detail, like specific aspects of our exes. This has allowed us to focus on building our relationship without unnecessary distractions.'

PART 2: THE ROLE OF BOUNDARIES AND EMOTIONAL PROTECTION

I. BOUNDARIES FOSTER PERSONAL AUTONOMY

- Maintaining personal autonomy within a relationship is crucial for emotional well-being. Carol Ryff's six dimensions of well-being (see page 17) emphasise the importance of autonomy as a key factor in a healthy relationship. Selective disclosure helps you maintain your own space while nurturing your connection with your partner.
- Example: 'By keeping certain thoughts and experiences private, I feel more in control of my own life, which has made me a better partner.'

2. PROTECT YOUR PARTNER'S EMOTIONAL WELL-BEING

- Before disclosing sensitive information, consider the emotional impact on your partner. If the information could cause harm without any constructive purpose, it might be better to keep it private. Sharing hurtful truths without considering the emotional outcome can damage trust and increase conflict.
- Example: 'I chose not to tell my partner about a brief crush I had because it would only cause unnecessary pain without improving our relationship.'

3. MANAGE PRIVACY THROUGH COMMUNICATION

- Communication Privacy Management theory highlights the importance of negotiating privacy boundaries in a relationship. By discussing what you both feel comfortable sharing and keeping private, you create a healthy balance of openness and personal space. This leads to better relationship satisfaction and trust.
- Example: 'We had a conversation about what topics were off-limits and agreed that certain aspects of our past relationships didn't need to be shared. This gave us both peace of mind.'

PART 3: THE DISCLOSURE CHECKLIST

I. SHARE WHAT'S RELEVANT

- Only disclose information that directly impacts your relationship. If it affects your daily life, shared goals or important decisions, it's worth sharing. Avoid sharing trivial or outdated details that don't add value to your relationship.
- Example: 'I told my partner about a financial decision I made because it affected our budget, but I didn't feel the need to mention a minor disagreement I had with a friend.'

2. CONSIDER THE EMOTIONAL IMPACT

- Weigh up the emotional consequences of what you're about to disclose. If sharing something could cause unnecessary harm or distress without benefiting the relationship, reconsider whether it's worth bringing up.
- Example: 'I didn't tell my partner about a past mistake I made before we met, because it would only make them feel anxious without adding anything positive to our relationship.'

3. RESPECT BOUNDARIES

- Ensure that what you disclose builds trust and intimacy without violating your partner's boundaries. If your partner has explicitly stated that they don't want to know certain details, respect that.
- Example: 'We agreed early on that we wouldn't discuss certain details about our previous sexual encounters, and it's helped us to focus on our own relationship instead of getting stuck in the past.'

4. CHOOSE THE RIGHT MOMENT

- Timing is key when sharing sensitive information. Avoid discussing difficult topics during stressful or inopportune moments. Choose a time when both you and your partner can be fully present and receptive.

- Example: 'Instead of bringing up a difficult conversation right before bed, I waited until we had some quiet time together on the weekend.'

5. BE CONSTRUCTIVE, NOT HURTFUL
- Frame your honesty in a way that's constructive. Use 'I' statements (see page 34) and express your feelings instead of placing blame or criticism. Avoid sharing information that will only hurt your partner without serving a constructive purpose.
- Example: 'I expressed my frustration about a recurring issue by focusing on how it made me feel, rather than blaming my partner.'

CONCLUSION

Full transparency is not always the healthiest approach in a relationship. Selective disclosure helps you to maintain personal autonomy, respect boundaries and protect emotional well-being while fostering trust and intimacy. By practising mindful disclosure, you can strengthen your relationship while avoiding unnecessary conflict.

TAKEAWAY

Choose what to share thoughtfully, balancing honesty with emotional protection. Use the disclosure checklist to guide your decisions, focusing on what's relevant and beneficial to your relationship. Selective disclosure will allow you to maintain personal boundaries while deepening your connection with your partner.

'FULFILLING,
RESPONSIVE DESIRE
NATURALLY LEADS
TO MORE SPONTANEITY'

MYTH 18

WITHOUT SPONTANEOUS DESIRE, YOUR RELATIONSHIP IS DOOMED TO FAIL

Provocative Truth: Sexual chemistry is not the key to long-term compatibility

Many people believe that spontaneity should be innate as a result of your physical attraction to your partner. But it is my contention that it is responsive desire that is the true foundation of a fulfilling and enduring relationship. Spontaneity is ultimately irrelevant.

The need to be spontaneous is reminiscent of the surface-level connection of sex without emotional intimacy that I spoke about in Chapter 6. You need a deeper emotional connection to feel comfortable to carve out time to be in the moment with your partner. The strength of your emotional intimacy is what begets sexual desire. And sexual desire is what can then lead to spontaneity. But just because you have strong sexual desire doesn't mean that you'll always be spontaneous. As the pressures and responsibilities of life mount with age, the opportunities to be spontaneous diminish. But this can be overcome if you have built up and sustained emotional intimacy and instead prioritise responsive desire.

WHAT IS RESPONSIVE DESIRE?

The concept of responsive desire originated from a researcher named Rosemary Basson, who argued that it is a form of desire that arises in response to sexual stimuli or a conducive context.[1] So, responsive desire is when a couple or one partner becomes sexually aroused through intimate actions and emotional connection, rather than just the urge for sex. Dr Karen Gurney took this concept further by incorporating it with the idea of emotional currency, which is made up of all the exchanges that you're making with your partner — the emotional intimacy, the strong communication, the feeling of safety and everything else that happens outside of having sex. This currency is what drives responsive desire, and this is truly the key to sustaining and growing long-term relationship sexual satisfaction.

One study broke down responsive desire into age groups: in the eighteen-to-twenty-nine bracket, 20 per cent of men prioritised responsive desire compared to 80 per cent who favoured spontaneous desire; between ages thirty and thirty-nine, the split was 25 per cent to 75 per cent; between forty and forty-nine it was 30 per cent to 70 per cent; between fifty and fifty-nine it was 35 per cent to 65 per cent; and sixty plus it was 40 per cent to 60 per cent.[2] This means that for men of all ages, there are a majority who emphasise spontaneous desire. But when you look at women, it's a completely different story. The split between responsive and spontaneous desire in women aged eighteen to twenty-nine is 30 per cent to 70 per cent; between thirty and thirty-nine it is 40 per cent to 60 per cent (meaning it is already in alignment with men 60 years old and above); between forty and forty-nine it's 50 – 50; between fifty and fifty-nine it's 60 per cent to 40 per cent; and sixty plus it's 70 per cent to 30 per cent. And this applies to women across the spectrum of sexual relationships.

The researchers pointed to a number of reasons for this discrepancy between the sexes and ages, including hormonal changes, particularly around menopause, which can affect spontaneous sexual desire. The perception of emotional and relational stability that comes with long-term relationships also fosters a strong sense of responsive desire. If you believe that something is off, there's going to be less responsive desire. Personal growth and confidence are also factors. With age, many women gain a better understanding of their sexual preferences and needs, leading to more confident and satisfying sexual experiences driven by responsive desire. I also think the inverse of this has a part to play too, with reduced confidence around body image and the stresses of daily life minimising the importance of spontaneous desire. But, according to Basson, responsive desire is most prevalent among women, of whatever sexual orientation, especially as they age in relationships, because of hormonal changes.

If we have this fundamental difference in the way that people, regardless of gender or orientation, approach sex via spontaneous and responsive desire, how can we successfully navigate those different needs and approaches? First, it's about general awareness, which leads to challenging the sexual scripts created by societal and cultural expectations; for example, the man has to perform, or the woman should not be assertive, or your partner needs to have a certain type of body shape, or that real sex is penetrative sex. Dr Gurney and others have written about the fact that conforming to these types of rigid sexual scripts leads to bad and predictable sex and therefore to dissatisfaction, so it's important that we challenge them.

Another way to navigate a discrepancy between a preference for responsive versus spontaneous desire in your relationship is to prioritise emotional intimacy and connection. Dr Gurney's research shows that most women need to feel safe to enjoy intimacy and have a more satisfying sexual experience. So, fostering this sense of safety via emotional intimacy is key, especially as we get older.

Quality over quantity is also important. In her book *Mind the Gap*, Dr Gurney included what some people might think is a bold statement: sex once a year that is great is better than sex once a week that is bad. I thought that was a powerful way to articulate the truth that quality is much more important than quantity.

Dr Gurney is also a massive advocate for the role of solo sex in overall relationship satisfaction. There are a variety of reasons for this, but one of them is better self-awareness, as it allows you to communicate exactly what you want from your partner. This also speaks to the orgasm gap, whereby 95 per cent of men and women can reliably orgasm through masturbation, but only 65 per cent of women can orgasm through penetrative sex.[3] This is why it is important to focus on stimulation outside of intercourse for women.

More generally, I think scheduling sex can be beneficial, and Dr Gurney agrees. When I and others suggest this, the common pushback is that scheduling sex is a turn-off. And I do concede that you can't necessarily switch desire on and off, except perhaps during the honeymoon period. But scheduling sex does not mean turning sexual desire on at the flick of a switch when the allotted hour arrives. Instead, you're making the space to be in the moment with your partner and prioritising sex in your relationship when there are so many other competing pulls on your time and attention. Furthermore, if you have done the work on creating emotional intimacy, it should be easier to be turned on when it is time to be sexually intimate, whatever that looks like for you and your partner, because you've created the conditions for responsive desire to build — you've already been turned on because of the strength of the emotional intimacy. Anticipation can also be a turn-on in and of itself, and there are, of course, many things that you could be doing preceding that moment. But the idea is that you feel safe with your partner and who you are.

SPONTANEITY CAN'T BE FORCED

It might be tempting to think that some sort of compromise is actually the way to balance spontaneous versus responsive desire, whereby if one partner tends to lean more towards the spontaneous side and their partner to the responsive, the spontaneous partner needs to create the environment to encourage a more responsive interaction, and the responsive partner has to try to inject spontaneity into their sex life. And there is something to be said for compromise in a relationship, but I tend towards the spontaneous partner needing to adapt to a more responsive form of desire, rather than the responsive partner having to become more spontaneous on demand, as, by its very nature, spontaneity can't be forced. I also believe that fulfilling, responsive desire naturally leads to more spontaneity. By being responsive and increasing the quality of interactions, the frequency will inevitably go up, and the spontaneity will increase too. To me, that's the key, as opposed to saying, 'You might not like this, and it might not be what gives you the most pleasure, but meet me halfway anyway.'

We saw in Chapter 6 that couples have sex on average three or four times per month, and that a greater frequency than this did not lead to any higher satisfaction. I think this also speaks to the importance of quality over quantity, and when partners can define their sexual interactions as high quality, that drives everything else, whether that be spontaneity or frequency.

It's also worth emphasising that a more responsive approach to desire is something that you can practise from an early age and stage in your relationship, and the more you go down that route, the more satisfaction you'll ultimately get. It's also beneficial to your relationship in general, because it promotes strong communication.

Emotional intelligence and putting somebody else's needs before your own are also relevant here, as thinking about what the other person wants is going to create that responsive environment. If you can do that, your own needs are likely to be met in a more satisfying way. As such, I would strongly advocate that you try to prioritise responsive over spontaneous desire, as it will lead to much more sustainable and fulfilling levels of intimacy in your relationship.

SELF-GUIDED INTERVENTION: EMBRACING RESPONSIVE DESIRE IN LONG-TERM RELATIONSHIPS

OBJECTIVE

To help you shift your focus from the myth of spontaneous desire being essential for a successful relationship to embracing responsive desire.

INTRODUCTION

Many people believe that spontaneous desire — the immediate, instinctual sexual attraction — is a necessary component of a thriving relationship. However, research and expert insights suggest that *responsive desire*, the desire that grows in response to emotional intimacy and connection, is key to long-term relationship satisfaction. The goal of this intervention is to help you and your partner to embrace the power of responsive desire, allowing you to strengthen your connection both sexually and emotionally. Responsive desire is not something that happens naturally all the time, especially as relationships mature. Unlike spontaneous desire, which is driven by physical attraction or novelty, responsive desire builds through emotional closeness, safety and mutual trust. By prioritising emotional intimacy, communication and quality of interaction, you and your partner can foster more fulfilling and sustainable sexual and emotional bonds.

PART I: UNDERSTANDING RESPONSIVE DESIRE

I. DEFINE RESPONSIVE DESIRE

- Responsive desire occurs when sexual interest is triggered in response to emotional and physical intimacy, rather than arising spontaneously. It's often fuelled by feeling emotionally connected and secure with your partner. Dr Rosemary Basson and Dr Karen Gurney have emphasised that responsive desire is a natural and important part of long-term relationships, particularly as partners age and experience changes in their physical or emotional needs.

- Example: 'I may not always feel spontaneous sexual desire, but after spending quality time together and feeling emotionally close, I'm more inclined to want intimacy with my partner.'

2. QUALITY OVER QUANTITY

- Dr Gurney suggests that the quality of sexual encounters is far more important than frequency (see Chapter 6). This means that prioritising meaningful, fulfilling sexual experiences — whether they happen once a week or once a month — will enhance satisfaction more than frequent but unsatisfying sex.

- Example: 'We've learned that it's not about how often we have sex but how connected we feel when we do.'

3. EMOTIONAL CURRENCY AND SEXUAL DESIRE

- Emotional currency refers to the small daily interactions that build emotional intimacy, such as thoughtful gestures, active listening and expressing affection. These actions create a sense of safety and trust, which fuels responsive desire. The more emotional currency you build, the more likely it is that desire will arise.

- Example: 'By focusing on being kind and thoughtful every day, we've noticed that our emotional connection leads to more spontaneous moments of intimacy.'

PART 2: CREATING THE CONDITIONS FOR RESPONSIVE DESIRE

I. PUT EMOTIONAL INTIMACY FIRST

- Prioritise emotional intimacy to cultivate an environment where responsive desire can flourish. This means being emotionally available, listening actively (see page 32) and validating each other's feelings.
- Example: 'We've started setting aside time to talk about how we're feeling emotionally, which has deepened our connection and increased our desire for one another.'

2. PRACTISE VULNERABILITY

- Responsive desire often stems from feeling safe and vulnerable with your partner. Sharing your feelings, insecurities and fears with one another will help foster a sense of emotional intimacy that enhances sexual desire.
- Example: 'We've learned that by being open about our vulnerabilities, we build trust, and that trust naturally leads to a deeper physical connection.'

3. SCHEDULE INTIMACY

- Although it may seem a bit contrived, scheduling intimate moments can be rewarding. By setting aside time to connect physically, you create an environment in which responsive desire can emerge naturally. Anticipation can build excitement and deepen the emotional connection.
- Example: 'Scheduling intimate time together has allowed us to prioritise each other amid our busy lives, leading to more meaningful and connected encounters.'

PART 3: CHALLENGING THE MYTH OF SPONTANEOUS DESIRE

I. REDEFINE SEXUAL SCRIPTS

- Many people are influenced by rigid cultural scripts that dictate how sex 'should' happen. These scripts often emphasise spontaneous sexual desire as the ideal. Instead, redefine these scripts to fit the reality of your relationship, prioritising emotional connection and quality over spontaneity.
- Example: 'We used to feel pressured to have spontaneous sex, but now we focus on creating moments of connection that lead to desire naturally.'

2. REJECT PERFORMANCE PRESSURE

- Performance anxiety and pressure to be spontaneous often hinder the natural development of desire. By focusing on emotional connection and quality interactions, you remove these pressures and create a more relaxed and enjoyable experience.
- Example: 'We've stopped putting pressure on ourselves to be spontaneous and instead focus on enjoying the time we spend together, which has led to more authentic moments of desire.'

PART 4: PRACTICAL TECHNIQUES TO FOSTER RESPONSIVE DESIRE

I. SCHEDULE EMOTIONAL CHECK-INS

- Regularly set aside time to talk about your feelings, needs and desires. Emotional check-ins create a deeper understanding of one another and build the foundation for responsive desire.
- Example: 'We have a weekly check-in where we talk about how we're doing emotionally. This has brought us closer and increased our desire for one another.'

2. CREATE RITUALS OF CONNECTION

- Develop daily or weekly rituals that foster emotional closeness, such as cooking dinner together, going for walks or practising mindfulness exercises as a couple.

- Example: 'We've started a nightly ritual of sharing one thing we appreciated about each other during the day, which has helped us stay connected and build intimacy.'

3. PRIORITISE NON-SEXUAL PHYSICAL TOUCH

- Engage in regular non-sexual physical affection, such as cuddling, holding hands or giving one another massages. This creates physical closeness without pressure, allowing desire to build naturally.
- Example: 'We've made an effort to cuddle more without any expectations, and this has led to a stronger connection and more frequent moments of intimacy.'

4. PRACTISE GRATITUDE AND APPRECIATION

- Expressing gratitude and appreciation for your partner strengthens emotional intimacy. Acknowledging the little things your partner does for you will help to maintain emotional connection and increase responsive desire.
- Example: 'Every day, I make a point to thank my partner for something they did, which has created a stronger bond between us.'

CONCLUSION

Responsive desire, not spontaneous desire, is the key to long-term relationship satisfaction. By focusing on emotional intimacy and non-sexual physical touch, you and your partner can foster an environment in which desire flourishes naturally. This shift allows you to build deeper emotional connections, experience more fulfilling sexual encounters and maintain a healthier and more sustainable relationship.

TAKEAWAY

Rather than chasing spontaneous desire, embrace the beauty of responsive desire. Prioritise emotional intimacy, practise vulnerability and create a foundation of trust that leads to a more satisfying, meaningful connection.

'IF BOTH PARTNERS
CAN'T FIND JOY OUTSIDE
OF THE RELATIONSHIP,
THINGS CAN BECOME
STAGNANT WITHIN IT'

MYTH 19

IT'S UNHEALTHY TO BE HAPPY WHEN SPENDING TIME APART FROM YOUR PARTNER

Provocative Truth: Prioritising personal interests and
fulfilment is essential for a healthy, growing relationship

I recently had to go to Paris for a couple of days for work, and Jill said to me before I went, 'I bet you can't wait to get out of here and sleep in a bed to yourself and spend some time on your own.' My immediate reaction was, 'No, what are you talking about? Of course I'm not happy to be going away.' It then dawned on me that I was buying into the myth that we shouldn't want to spend time apart from our partners, and that if you're happy or fulfilled when doing so, it means there's a lack of commitment or love. The implication is that true happiness should only be found within a relationship, and if you find any joy independent of that, it's a sign of an unhealthy relationship.

This myth is firmly embedded in popular culture. I'm not proud to admit it, but, until 2024, I had never seen or read *Romeo and Juliet*. I then went to see the production starring Tom Holland and, despite what some of the critics had to say, I thought it was phenomenal. I love Shakespeare and have seen lots of his plays in person, but I was blown away. It was obvious why it is considered to be one of our most timeless love stories. But it also supports this myth, because Romeo and Juliet are completely dependent on one another's love to the exclusion of all others. And this ideal has been perpetuated in literature and drama ever since.

THE IMPORTANCE OF OUTSIDE INTERESTS

One of the downsides to believing in this myth is that it increases the pressure and stress on your relationship if you think your partner should be your only source of happiness. It might also lead to you losing some of your personal identity, because you lose sight of your own interests and independence as sources of happiness and fulfilment, which can, in turn, stunt your relationship growth. And if both partners can't find joy outside of the relationship, things can become stagnant within it. If you become so insular and don't tap into any outside influences, codependence can be the outcome and, at the most extreme end of the spectrum, even premature death.

The latter is known as the 'widowhood effect', or 'broken heart syndrome', which is the increased probability of a surviving spouse dying shortly after their partner's death. This has been backed up by research that shows the risk of mortality spikes when your partner dies.[1] A famous example of this is Johnny Cash and his wife June Carter. They were married and performed together for thirty-five years and, although their relationship had its issues, they were known to be an incredibly loving couple. Then, in 2003, June Carter passed away unexpectedly. Johnny Cash died four months later. In those four months, he recorded in the region of sixty songs, having told the record producer Rick Rubin, 'You have to keep me working because I will die if I don't have something to do.'[2] Despite doing this work, he didn't really step outside of his house, and he wasn't as plugged in to his social circle. And although his health wasn't great anyway, it is hard not to see some link between the heartache he was feeling at losing the partner whom he had been so dependent on and his own death not long afterwards.

As we get older, we have shrinking social circles and decreased self-care. A Centers for Disease Control and Prevention study found that only 28 per cent of adults aged seventy-five or older engaged in any regular activity.[3] We also have increased health issues, with 80 per cent of older adults suffering from at least one chronic disease. Then there is social isolation, with an American Association of Retired Persons study showing that 35 per cent of adults aged forty-five or older consider themselves to be lonely.[4] A lack of social connections leads to fewer opportunities for recognition and validation of our own personal achievements. We also see a decline in the number of quality conversations we are having on a regular basis, which is not something that I see talked about as much when it comes to the impact of a shrinking social circle, but it is extremely important. A study published in *Psychological Science* found that engaging in deep conversations, as opposed to superficial small talk, on a regular basis has a positive impact on emotional well-being.[5] It was my father's birthday the other day, and it got me thinking about how the quality of his meaningful conversations is nowhere near what it used to be. This can lead to decreased emotional support if you don't have a partner, and more reliance on them if you do. This is why it is so important to cultivate interests beyond your relationship.

FINDING INTERESTS OUTSIDE OF YOUR RELATIONSHIP

Michelle and Barack Obama are my role models when it comes to partners who maintain a strong sense of independence outside of their relationship. Regardless of what you might think of their politics, they are always championing the importance of individual activities and pursuing things on their own. Michelle writes

books and campaigns for causes that are important to her, and
Barack still has his political pursuits, as well as spending a fair
amount of time on the golf course. In addition to enhanced
personal development growth, which leads to a more fulfilling life,
this has clear benefits for their marriage. When both partners are
independently happy, they bring positive energy and fresh experiences into the relationship. Knowing that it's OK to be happy when
spending time apart also reduces the pressure on the relationship,
because it no longer has to be the sole source of your joy, which
means that you're more relaxed and have a healthier dynamic.
Having strong outside interests can also improve communication, because, when you spend time apart, you have more to talk
about and share.

I keep coming back to the fact that you need to work on yourself first, and it's about personal growth and individual well-being
before relationship well-being. So, if you're in a relationship and
you don't really have any outside interests or spend any time apart
from your partner, then you need to focus on those things and
work on increasing your personal well-being. One way of doing
this, although I acknowledge that it probably sounds a bit basic
and obvious, is to find an individual hobby and pursue things
outside of your relationship that give you joy.

Thinking back to the wife of our friend who died, some people
might have thought the fact that she was going to spas and well-
ness retreats, and then after a while started dating again, somehow undermined her feelings for him: 'Why is she out here? It
looks like she's living her best life. She must never have loved
him.' But it soon dawned on me that that wasn't right. Because
she had a high level of personal well-being in the relationship, she
already had all of these sources of joy in her life that she was able
to plug in to; she didn't have to create or find them.

That was when I started to think, 'I really need to find joy
outside of my relationship, because I spend 99.9 per cent of my

time when I am not working with my family.' I knew that I had to figure out how to tap in to other sources. And I think this is an incredibly important lesson for many men, because our mortality rates are much higher when our partners pass away, as demonstrated by the widowhood effect.

I was always taught and grew up believing that the key to a successful relationship is to spend all of your time with your partner and family if you have one. As a result, I really narrowed my social network — for example, I used to watch American football with my friends on Sundays, but, over time, I slowly extracted myself from doing those sorts of things, thinking that it was a net positive to my relationship, and there were benefits to it. But now, as I'm older, I realise that I put myself in a detrimental position by shrinking and removing myself from my social network, as it lessened my autonomy, which diminished my all-round well-being.

Because I wasn't someone who really had interests outside of work and family, I had to find some hobbies. My latest is getting involved with a local football team. It probably sounds like a huge flex, but the other night one of my boys sent me a link to a football manager app, and I replied, 'I don't need an app. I'm doing that for real now.' My involvement with the team is a healthy outlet for me.

This is backed up by the research. A study on self-determination theory shows that you need autonomy and self-determined behaviour to support your overall well-being.[6] In other words, personal happiness is crucial for a healthy relationship, and you can't have that unless you have some semblance of autonomy. Another study, by researchers Berkman and Glass, which looked into social integration, social networks and social support, stressed the importance of having support networks outside of romantic relationships for high well-being and good overall health.[7]

Celebrating independence is also very important, and that's something that Jill and I try to do as a couple, although it's not always easy. Jill recently decided that she wanted to learn how to swim and found an incredible residential crash course that teaches you in a week. Although it was something she'd always wanted to do, I could tell she was reluctant to go, and not because she was fearful of going or of the swimming. She was worried about leaving for seven days — perhaps she thought I was going to blow up the house without her being there to keep an eye on us — but I encouraged her to sign up. Then, a few days before it was due to start, she suggested that we all go together. I said, 'No, you should do this. You'll have a great time, and we'll be OK.' Figuring out how to celebrate and speak the importance of this kind of independence into your relationship is important.

Setting boundaries and respecting them is again important here. Some couples are like Velcro, which is one extreme, and others hardly spend any time with one another at all, which is the other. Finding a balance is important, and working within the expectations of both partners means that one won't be upset if the other decides to spend a bit more time pursuing their own interests outside of the relationship. It's not about neglecting your relationship or neglecting your partner. It's about finding outlets beyond the relationship.

It's also about being able to identify goals that you are pursuing independent of your relationship, and personal development involves acquiring the skills required to reach those goals. This requires time, energy, focus and resources, but it's well worth it. Time is precious and, for some couples, there might be financial or other drains on their resources that make it difficult, but you have to carve out the time and allocate the resources to do this, because otherwise it's going to be detrimental to your relationship. And there are hobbies that don't cost money or are relatively inexpensive, such as walking groups, birdwatching or wild swimming.

WHAT ABOUT WORK AS AN OUTLET?

A distinction can be made between having outside interests and your work life being separate from your relationship. A lot of us pour a lot of our time and effort into work, and it's a world apart from our partners (unless you work with them, of course), but it doesn't give you the sort of benefits of self-autonomy that I've been recommending unless you can say that it is something that brings you joy. If it does, and it allows you to plug in to and inter-act with a different network, and helps you to develop skills that can be brought to bear in a positive way on your relationship, then these are pluses when it comes to your well-being, and it is therefore beneficial.

I think that's one of the reasons for empty-nest syndrome and the rise in relationships falling apart when people reach retire-ment age. If you have one partner who's removed themselves from the workplace and dramatically reduced their network as a result of that, while the other has continually engaged with outside interests, it's not surprising that you might get conflict or one partner feeling that they have outgrown the other. That is particularly the case if the work was especially meaningful to the person who now finds themselves without purpose and direction.

The depth of the work relationships you cultivate is also important. In a lot of work environments, the connections are not extraordinarily deep, and conversation tends towards the superfi-cial. But if you're in a work environment where the connections go a bit deeper than the superficial, that's a plus.

Berkman and Glass also argue that any network, in which-ever environment, is helpful as long as it's diverse and active.[8] It being diverse is important because it's the diversity that creates new ideas, which is ultimately the point of spending time apart — stopping things from becoming stale and stagnant. Again, my involvement with the football club is a good case in point, as it is a totally new network for me. It will be something different for you, but whatever it is, make sure you are ring-fencing time for it, as it's not selfish or frivolous to do things on your own — it is essential if you want your relationship to thrive in the long term.

SELF-GUIDED INTERVENTION: EMBRACING INDEPENDENCE AND TIME APART IN RELATIONSHIPS

OBJECTIVE

To encourage you to embrace time apart from your partner and pursue individual interests, enhancing personal well-being and strengthening relationship satisfaction.

INTRODUCTION

There is a common belief that partners should spend all their time together, and that any time apart indicates a lack of commitment or love. Many fear that enjoying time away from their partner means the relationship is lacking something. However, research and experience show that pursuing individual interests and having time apart can actually benefit a relationship by fostering personal growth, reducing stress and allowing each partner to bring new experiences and energy into the relationship. This intervention will guide you in understanding the benefits of time apart, fostering personal growth, establishing healthy boundaries and how individual pursuits can contribute to long-term relationship satisfaction.

PART I: UNDERSTANDING THE BENEFITS OF TIME APART

I. REDUCE RELATIONSHIP PRESSURE

- The myth that partners should be one another's only source of happiness increases pressure on the relationship. By finding joy outside the relationship, you reduce this pressure and create space for both partners to grow individually.

- Example: 'We've learned that by pursuing our own interests, we feel less pressure to fulfil one another's every need, which makes us happier as individuals and as a couple.'

2. AVOID CODEPENDENCE

- Relying solely on your partner for happiness can lead to codependence, where personal identity becomes lost and relationship growth stalls. Time apart allows you to maintain your own sense of self and prevents emotional stagnation.
- Example: 'When I started taking time to pursue my own interests, I realised how much more confident and fulfilled I felt, and that confidence improved my relationship.'

3. ENHANCE PERSONAL WELL-BEING

- Pursuing your own interests, whether through hobbies, work or social activities, is essential for personal well-being. Studies show that having a diverse and active social network outside of a romantic relationship contributes to higher well-being.
- Example: 'Joining a local running group gave me a chance to build new friendships, and it's had a positive impact on my mood and energy levels, which I bring back into my relationship.'

PART 2: FINDING JOY IN INDEPENDENCE

I. PURSUE HOBBIES OR PASSIONS

- Find an activity or hobby that you enjoy and dedicate time to it. Whether it's a sport, creative pursuit or social activity, having something outside your relationship that brings you joy will improve your mental health and bring fresh energy into your partnership.
- Example: 'I took up photography, and not only did it give me personal satisfaction, but sharing my experiences with my partner created new conversations and brought us closer.'

2. MAINTAIN A STRONG SOCIAL NETWORK

- Friends and social connections outside of your romantic relationship are essential. They provide emotional support, perspective and opportunities for personal growth. Cultivate and nurture these relationships, as they are crucial for overall life satisfaction.
- Example: 'I made it a priority to reconnect with friends I hadn't seen in a while. Having that social time outside of my relationship has given me a sense of balance and support.'

3. SUPPORT YOUR PARTNER'S INDEPENDENCE

- Encourage your partner to pursue their interests and passions as well. This can be a key part of maintaining balance in a relationship and preventing one partner from feeling neglected or trapped. Celebrate each other's independence.
- Example: 'When my partner wanted to sign up for a yoga retreat, I encouraged them to go, knowing it would benefit their well-being, and when they returned, we had more to share and bond over.'

PART 3: BALANCING TIME TOGETHER AND APART
I. SET BOUNDARIES AND EXPECTATIONS

- It's important to discuss and set boundaries around time apart so that both you and your partner feel secure. Knowing that time apart is a healthy and intentional part of the relationship helps prevent misunderstandings and feelings of neglect.
- Example: 'We agreed that one weekend a month we'd each do something on our own, whether it's seeing friends or engaging in our hobbies. This has helped us to stay connected without feeling smothered.'

2. CREATE RITUALS FOR CONNECTION

- While time apart is important, it's equally important to create rituals for connection when you are together. This ensures that you maintain emotional intimacy and support one another's growth.

- Example: 'We make sure to have a special dinner once a week where we talk about our individual experiences from the past week, which helps us stay connected and invested in one another's lives.'

3. RECOGNISE THE VALUE OF SOLITUDE

- Spending time alone is valuable for personal reflection and growth. It can help you process your emotions, think about your goals and recharge. This self-awareness and self-care ultimately strengthens your ability to show up fully in your relationship.
- Example: 'Taking time for myself to reflect and decompress has made me more present and engaged when I am with my partner.'

PART 4: NAVIGATING CHALLENGES
I. OVERCOME GUILT ABOUT ENJOYING TIME APART

- Many people feel guilty or anxious about enjoying time apart from their partner. It's important to reframe this as a healthy part of maintaining a fulfilling relationship. Being happy on your own doesn't diminish your love or commitment.
- Example: 'I used to feel guilty when I enjoyed time with friends away from my partner, but now I realise that those experiences make me happier and more appreciative of my relationship.'

2. COMMUNICATION AND REASSURANCE

- It's natural for partners to feel insecure when the other spends time apart. Open communication is key — reassure your partner that your time apart is about personal growth, not a reflection of dissatisfaction in the relationship.
- Example: 'We regularly check in with one another to make sure that our time apart feels balanced and beneficial for both of us. This open dialogue has strengthened our trust.'

CONCLUSION

Spending time apart and pursuing individual interests is not only healthy but essential for the well-being of both you and your partner, and the relationship as a whole. This independence fosters personal growth, reduces pressure on the relationship and brings fresh energy and experiences into your partnership, leading to greater relationship satisfaction.

TAKEAWAY

Rather than seeing time apart as a threat to your relationship, view it as a necessary tool for growth and fulfilment. Embrace independence, support your partner's pursuits and find the balance that works for your relationship. By doing so, you'll create a more enriching, satisfying partnership.

'THE BEST
RELATIONSHIPS
EVOLVE – THEY ARE
NEVER STATIC'

MYTH 20

THE NOTION OF 'SOULMATES' IS FUNDAMENTAL TO ROMANTIC SUCCESS

Provocative Truth: There is no such thing as a perfect partner, and 'soulmates' are never found – they are made through realistic expectations and growth together

The idea that you have a 'soulmate', or one person who completes you, is a compelling one, as it suggests that, when you find your perfect partner, it'll lead to everlasting happiness and effortless love. It's rooted in the belief that a soulmate is someone who is made for you and will fulfil all of your emotional needs. And when you have found that person, there will be an immediate, deep connection, and it won't require work to maintain the relationship.

So, where does this idea come from? As with a lot of myths, you have to go back to Ancient Greece. In Plato's *The Symposium*, dating from circa 385 to 370 BCE, a range of notable figures at a banquet give a series of speeches. Aristophanes, the comic playwright, tells a story about the origin of human beings, which he explains were originally creatures with four arms, four legs and a single head with two faces looking in opposite directions. There were three combinations: all female, all male and a male and female mix. These beings were incredibly powerful — so powerful, in fact, that they attempted to challenge the gods. Zeus quashed the rebellion, but he did not wish to lose their offerings, so instead of destroying them, he decided to weaken them by splitting them in half, creating two separate individuals. Humans were left feeling incomplete and have been perpetually searching for their other halves to restore their original wholeness ever since. This is where the idea of the missing half, or soulmate, comes from, and it gathered steam as the centuries passed, to the point that many of us today are still looking for someone to complete us — a concept that popular culture has done much to reinforce.

In addition, there are a number of other reasons why people believe this myth outside of the cultural narratives that we are all familiar with. The first is psychological comfort — the idea that there is a perfect person for you provides comfort and reassurance in a world that's so uncertain. It's also a part of many religious and spiritual beliefs, which often espouse the idea that relationships are preordained and souls are meant to reunite. That's why in the past you had to go to the church for your relationship to be sanctioned. In essence, what the church was doing was saying that, yes, this is the partner who was meant for you, and the vows underscored that you were with someone who you were supposed to share the rest of your life with.

BELIEVING IN SOULMATES PROMOTES A FIXED MINDSET

Believing in soulmates can cause you to overlook potential matches in the first place, as you could have a tendency to dismiss compatible partners who might not fit your idealised notion of perfection. Then, when you are in a relationship, the idea of a perfect match can lead to unrealistic expectations, which can create disillusionment and disappointment. Also, when conflicts arise and challenges pop up, you are liable to think that you're with the wrong person. This means that you are less likely to want to do the work to solve the issue, which can then lead to the relationship falling apart.

The research backs this up. One study found that individuals who believe in soulmates tend to avoid addressing conflict directly, as they see conflict as a sign of incompatibility rather than a normal aspect of a relationship. Their findings showed that 68 per cent of individuals who believed in soulmates reported avoiding conflict to maintain harmony, compared to 45 per cent of those with a growth mindset in the relationship.[1] Another study found that people who subscribe to the theory of soulmates are more likely to terminate relationships prematurely, believing significant conflicts indicate that they're not true soulmates, with 55 per cent of soulmate believers ending their relationships over significant conflict versus 30 per cent who believed in relationship growth.[2] And another study found that a belief in soulmates correlated with lower relationship satisfaction due to unmet high expectations. Couples with high self-efficacy reported 20 per cent higher relationship satisfaction than those who believed in a soulmate, and 40 per cent lower relationship satisfaction was reported among soulmate believers compared to those who focused on relationship growth.[3] I believe Carol Dweck's theory of fixed and growth mindsets applies here.[4] Those with a fixed mindset believe qualities like compatibility are set in stone, which can lead to them avoiding challenges and giving up when conflicts arise. In contrast, those with a growth mindset view challenges as opportunities for development and improvement. In relationships, the latter mindset fosters resilience and long-term success, as partners see conflict not as a sign of failure but as a chance to grow together.

So, believing in soulmates is restrictive when it comes to trying to find a partner in the first place — it's much more difficult to find the right person if you are looking for one in 7 billion — but it also has a really negative impact on an ongoing basis once you're in the relationship because of the false expectations and fixed mindset it promotes.

EMBRACING RELATIONSHIP GROWTH

The truth is that you need to encourage and develop a more realistic approach to relationship compatibility. It's about mutual respect, and it's about communication. Most importantly, it's about recognising that relationships develop and grow just as much as individuals do. A soulmate implies a finished product, but there is no such thing as perfection, and the best relationships evolve — they are never static. I often hear platitudes such as, 'She made me feel like I could walk on air,' but that suggests infatuation, another by-product of the soulmate myth that has nothing to do with true compatibility, well-being or a high level of satisfaction in your relationship. The concept of a soulmate does nothing to advance knowledge or discernment of whether or not someone can help to deliver relationship satisfaction. In fact, it can do the opposite, as it shuts down any opportunity for conflict or more in-depth emotional connection, and it does not allow you to grow as a couple.

Many of the myths in this book revolve around the pursuit of perfection, but perfection doesn't exist, and aiming for it can be damaging. There's been a shift since the 1960s and '70s to today's mindset that if someone isn't 100 per cent perfect or doesn't meet every expectation, they should be dismissed. This approach is dangerous, as it overlooks the potential for growth within a relationship. Instead of searching for a flawless partner, we should focus on growing and evolving together, embracing imperfections as opportunities for deepening connection.

The idea of a soulmate is quite Western-centric. In contrast, arranged marriages in some cultures have shown that relationships can grow and flourish over time, even without the idea of a 'perfect match'. That said, the East is now also experiencing a shift towards individualism, especially in urban areas of Japan, South Korea and China, where family involvement in relationship decisions is diminishing, leading to social upheaval. As a result, some of the strongest counter-narratives to traditional relationship models are emerging from this part of the world. One example is South Korea's '4B' (Four Nos) movement: a radical feminist philosophy that rejects having sex with men, dating men, marrying men and giving birth, reflecting a rejection of patriarchal values. This movement highlights the shift from collectivism towards individualism, paralleling the rise in the West of the soulmate ideal. Yet, true relational success isn't found in a perfect partner, but in growing together through challenges and cultivating a dynamic relationship that evolves over time. And that is true whatever part of the world you live in.

SELF-GUIDED INTERVENTION: REFRAMING THE SOULMATE MYTH AND EMBRACING RELATIONSHIP GROWTH

OBJECTIVE

To help you move beyond the limiting belief in soulmates and foster a growth-oriented mindset in your relationship.

INTRODUCTION

The idea of a soulmate is alluring, promising effortless love and a deep connection with one perfect person. However, this notion can lead to unrealistic expectations and disappointment when conflicts inevitably arise. The truth is that no partner is perfect, and the strongest relationships are those where both partners grow together, embracing challenges and changes. This intervention aims to reframe the soulmate myth and introduce practices that foster personal growth, communication, realistic expectations, mutual respect and resilience, all of which contribute to long-term relationship satisfaction.

PART I: UNDERSTANDING THE SOULMATE MYTH

I. RECOGNISE THE MYTH

- Reflect by asking yourself if you have ever felt that you needed to find a 'perfect' partner to be truly happy. If the answer is yes, how did this belief shape your approach to dating or your current relationship?
- The soulmate myth suggests there is one perfect person who will complete you. This belief is rooted in both ancient philosophy and modern pop culture, but it overlooks the fact that relationships require effort, communication and mutual growth.
- Example: 'For years, I believed in the idea of a perfect partner who would meet all of my emotional needs. This caused me to reject many potential partners because I thought they weren't "the one". It took me time to realise that a great relationship doesn't have to be perfect from the start.'

2. THE IMPACT OF THE SOULMATE MYTH ON RELATIONSHIPS

- Believing in soulmates can cause individuals to:
  - » Overlook potential partners because they don't fit an idealised vision.
  - » Avoid working through conflicts, seeing them as signs of incompatibility rather than normal relationship challenges.
  - » End relationships prematurely when they don't meet high expectations.
- Activity: Reflect on a past relationship that ended due to unmet expectations. Were these expectations realistic or were they shaped by the belief in finding a 'perfect' match?

- Example: 'Looking back, I realise I ended a relationship because I felt like we didn't connect deeply enough from the start. Now I understand that relationships take time to grow.'

PART 2: EMBRACING A GROWTH MINDSET IN RELATIONSHIPS
I. SHIFT FROM A FIXED TO A GROWTH MINDSET

- A fixed mindset believes that compatibility is set in stone and that a perfect match requires no effort. A growth mindset sees challenges as opportunities for development and connection.
- Activity: Reflect on an ongoing challenge in your relationship. How could approaching it with a growth mindset help improve your dynamic?
- Example: 'My partner and I have different communication styles, and this has caused frustration in the past. Instead of thinking we're incompatible, I'm working on seeing this as an opportunity for us to grow in how we express our needs.'

2. FOCUS ON RELATIONSHIP GROWTH

- The idea of a soulmate can make us overlook the importance of evolving together. Real relationships grow through mutual respect, good communication and working through conflicts. No one is a perfect partner from the start; mutual growth leads to deeper compatibility.
- Ask yourself how your relationship has evolved over time and what strengths you have developed as a couple.
- Example: 'At the beginning of our relationship, we had different ideas about spending time together. Over the years, we've learned how to balance our needs and become more in tune with one another's preferences.'

PART 3: RELATIONSHIP JOURNALING AS A TOOL FOR GROWTH

I. THE POWER OF JOURNALING

- Relationship journaling is a great tool for developing a growth mindset. Both you and your partner reflect on a specific prompt related to your relationship, write about it for ten minutes and then share your thoughts. This helps address underlying issues, build positive reinforcement and promote self-awareness and mutual understanding.

- Activity: Set a weekly or monthly journaling session with your partner. Choose a prompt from the list below, write freely for ten minutes and then spend ten minutes discussing your thoughts. Keep the conversation positive and focused on growth.

- Example: 'We have started to use prompts to reflect on what we most appreciate about one another each week. This has deepened our connection and allowed us to express things that sometimes go unsaid in the rush of daily life.'

Suggested journaling prompts for growth

- Prompt 1: In what respect would you say that your relationship has grown the most in the past year?

- Prompt 2: Describe a recent challenge you've faced as a couple. How did you handle it and what did you learn from the experience?

- Prompt 3: What do you most appreciate about your partner today that you didn't notice when you first started dating?

- Prompt 4: How has your understanding of love and commitment evolved since you entered this relationship?

- Prompt 5: What are some ways you can continue to grow as individuals while supporting one another's personal growth?

PART 4: REFRAMING EXPECTATIONS

I. REALISE THERE IS NO PERFECT PARTNER

- Understanding that no one person can meet all your needs is freeing. A strong relationship is based on realistic expectations, mutual growth and support, not on finding someone who fulfils every emotional, intellectual or physical need.
- Activity: Make a list of your top five expectations in a partner. Reflect on which ones are essential for a successful relationship and which might be based on unrealistic ideals.
- Example: 'I used to think my partner needed to share all my interests. Now I see that it's more important that we respect one another's differences and support our individual passions.'

2. BUILD A RELATIONSHIP FOCUSED ON GROWTH

- A successful relationship isn't about finding someone who completes you; it's about building a life together where both you and your partner grow individually and as a couple.
- Reflect on how you can actively support your partner's growth and grow individually while enhancing your relationship.
- Example: 'We've started setting personal and relationship goals together, which helps us support each other while growing in our individual pursuits.'

Bonus: Journaling prompts for ongoing growth

- Prompt 1: What was a moment in your relationship that felt especially challenging? How did you grow through it?
- Prompt 2: How do you feel about the concept of soulmates now, compared to before starting this intervention?
- Prompt 3: In what ways do you contribute to the growth of your relationship? How does your partner contribute?
- Prompt 4: Reflect on a quality your partner has that you initially didn't appreciate but now see as a strength.

- Prompt 5: How do you think your relationship will continue to evolve in the next five years? What steps can you take to support that growth?

CONCLUSION

The concept of soulmates can lead to unrealistic expectations and disappointment. Instead, cultivating a growth mindset, whereby both you and your partner embrace challenges and opportunities to evolve together, is key to long-term relationship success. Through journaling, open communication and reframing expectations, you can create a stronger, more fulfilling partnership that adapts and grows over time.

THE INTERVENTION IN PRACTICE

Jill and I have benefited from relationship journaling, although it is something that we now do in a less formal, more everyday fashion. Because of the work that we do and our interest in relationships, every time one of us reads something interesting or discovers something new, we tell the other one about it. For example, Jill recently told me that the Philippines and Vatican City are the only two places in the world where divorce is illegal, which is something I never knew. This then acted as a prompt for a wider discussion about something that was relevant to our relationship. Sometimes the prompt might lead to a chat about what we most appreciate about one another this week, or something challenging that we went through, or something to do with our sex life. The whole point is that we have these prompts and then use them to discuss aspects of our relationship. It's less about addressing specific issues and more about promoting growth. I think of relationship journaling as more of a check-up, as opposed to something urgent that needs a visit to A&E. It should also be fun, it should be positive and it should lead to really meaningful interactions. If it hits all of these markers, you will see the benefit in no time, and it will be of help to you regardless of whether or not you tend towards the sort of fixed mindset suggested by a belief in soulmates.

TAKEAWAY

No partner is perfect, but every relationship has the potential for growth. Focus on building a dynamic relationship where you and your partner can evolve together, support each other's development and embrace the imperfections that come with real, lasting love.

'IF YOU HAVE A
SUCCESSFUL,
SATISFIED
PARTNERSHIP,
LONGEVITY WILL
BE A BY-PRODUCT
OF THAT'

MYTH 21

BELIEVING YOUR PARTNER WILL BE WITH YOU FOREVER HELPS YOUR RELATIONSHIP TO FLOURISH

Provocative Truth: Believing your partner will stay forever may seem romantic, but it can breed complacency and ignores the fact that relationships need constant effort, adaptation and growth

The notion that your partner will be with you forever, and your relationship is more likely to succeed as a result of that, is rooted in the idea that love is unbreakable, unshakeable and eternal. It is such a powerful idea that it has got to the point that longevity is by far the most common way by which we judge relationship success today.

And it is obvious why it is such an attractive concept, as thinking you are going to be together forever should, in theory, make your partner feel more secure and bonded to you, and you to them. But, as with all of these myths, the opposite is true in many cases. Feeling confident that your partner is going to be there forever can lead to you not wanting to put in any extra work, similar to the negative impact of believing in a soulmate.

We have been measuring the success of relationships in terms of their longevity for centuries. For example, the concept of a silver wedding anniversary dates back to the Holy Roman Empire in Germany in the Middle Ages, where husbands would present their wives with a silver wreath to commemorate twenty-five years of marriage, symbolising the value and durability of their relationship. This then developed and couples reaching fifty years of marriage were honoured with a gold wreath, the more precious metal symbolising the rarity of such an occasion at a time when average life expectancy was much lower.[1]

The association of diamonds with sixtieth anniversaries, meanwhile, dates back to Queen Victoria and the celebration of her diamond jubilee in 1897, marking her sixty years on the throne. This milestone was then adopted to celebrate sixty-year marriages, the diamonds symbolising strength and brilliance. The commercialisation of this landmark also entrenched it further in society, with the American National Retail Jeweler Association introducing an expanded list of anniversary gifts in 1937 to help market their products, including pearl, ruby and platinum anniversaries.[2]

But even before we began to mark wedding anniversaries by giving precious metals and stones, the importance of lasting union was promoted by religion. Within Christianity, for example, there are a number of passages that emphasise the permanence of married union, including, 'So then, they are no longer two but one flesh. Therefore what God has joined together, let not man separate' (Matthew 19:6), and the same sentiment is expressed in Mark 10, followed by a repudiation of divorce: 'So He said to them, "Whoever divorces his wife and marries another commits adultery against her. And if a woman divorces her husband and marries another, she commits adultery."'

You can find similar sentiments in the Hebrew Bible, or Tanakh, which makes up much of the Old Testament; for example, in Malachi 2:16 it says, 'For the Lord God of Israel says that He hates divorce, for it covers one's garment with violence.' And in the Quran 30:24 it says, 'And one of His signs is that He created for you spouses from among yourselves so that you may find comfort in them. And He has placed between you compassion and mercy.' The idea here is that mercy is the foundation for a stable family and society, highlighting the importance of maintaining the marital bond. In this way, religious teachings really cemented the idea of a relationship lasting forever.

The reasons for this are varied, but you could argue that the elevation of marriage and the creation of the nuclear family, particularly in Western cultures, was a means of expanding the influence of religion, diminishing the role of the clan and formalising processes such as inheritance. In other words, it was about controlling people. The consequences of this were wide-ranging, but one of the outcomes was a premium being placed on lifelong relationships.

You can also see this idea play out in wedding vows. 'Till death us do part' is one of the central components of a traditional Christian marriage ceremony, but the wedding vows of many other religions also include a reference to forever. In Hinduism, for example, the seventh and final vow is a prayer for lifelong love and friendship.[3] The groom promises, 'We are now husband and wife, and are one. You are mine and I am yours for eternity,' and the bride promises, 'As God is witness, I am now your wife. We will love, honour and cherish each other forever.' And while vows are not an essential part of an Islamic wedding, which is based around the Nikah, or marriage contract, many Muslims choose to incorporate vows into the ceremony based on the teachings of the Quran. A popular one is, 'I take you to be my wife or husband. We were once one soul, split in two, a perfect pair, and now we become one again in marriage. Today I pledge my loyalty and love to you for as long as we live, as your faithful husband or wife and constant friend.'[4] I think it's also interesting that both of these examples stress the coming together of two people to become one, also emphasising the religious foundations of the idea of soulmates that we explored in the previous chapter.

I think it is possible to respect the different cultural and religious narratives at play, but, at the same time, set realistic expectations within that framework. So, you might choose to commit to one another for the rest of your lives — 'till death us do part' — as a means of appreciating the cultural and religious aspect of the tradition within which you are getting married (if you are doing so in a religious context, although many secular ceremonies now include an element of forever too), but, at the same time, it's important to realise that the longevity of the relationship is not what you're really aiming for. If you have a successful, satisfied partnership, longevity will be a by-product of that, but it's not the ultimate goal. Again, relationship mentorship is a helpful way to gain this perspective.

Culture has also played its part. Every fairy tale — *Cinderella*, *Snow White*, *Sleeping Beauty*, you name it — ends with 'happily ever after', which encapsulates the notion of the protagonist overcoming great odds and finding eternal love. The origins of the phrase are uncertain, although it was ubiquitous in fairy tales from the nineteenth century onwards. The concept has stayed with us ever since, and we now see it in popular films — *Pretty Woman*, *The Notebook* and so on — and also in literature — the novels of Jane Austen spring immediately to mind — with the characters overcoming all obstacles to end up with one another and live happily ever after (even if that phrase is not used explicitly).

ENJOY THE JOURNEY

Believing that longevity is the best marker of a successful relationship brings with it a lot of negatives. First, it can lead to you not addressing conflict and problems, thinking that your relationship is strong enough to survive no matter what. You're together forever anyway, so maybe the issues will just go away if you ride it out. Second, it can cause stunted growth, with the relationship stagnating because the partners are not motivated to grow, adapt and improve their dynamic, leading to dissatisfaction over time. Third, believing your partner will be there forever can create a false sense of security, leading to complacency and taking each other for granted. When you assume 'forever', it's possible that you might stop putting in the effort to maintain and nurture the relationship. It can also lead to over-reliance on your partner to fulfil all of your needs, neglecting the importance of widening your social circle and seeking support from others. This not only strains the relationship, but also prevents personal growth and a healthy balance of external connections. Relationships require ongoing effort, adaptation and mutual growth. Without that, the assumption of forever can lead to stagnation.

A much better marker of relationship success is satisfaction in the moment. It's about enjoying the journey, not the destination. This is something that I've repeatedly talked about and tried to practise in my own life and relationship. Psychological research supports this approach, showing that couples who focus on day-to-day satisfaction are more likely to have lasting, fulfilling relationships than those who fixate on long-term guarantees. One study found that savouring positive moments together fosters stronger emotional bonds.[5]

In addition to this psychological evidence, there's also a lot of philosophical thinking that supports living in the moment and prioritising the process over the outcome. For instance, Alan

Watts's analogy that life is more like a dance or a musical performance, where the point is to enjoy the process rather than trying
to reach an end goal, comes to mind. To me, that's a fantastic way
to describe a good life and a good relationship, whether platonic or
romantic. Figuring out how to appreciate and take satisfaction in
the moment versus prioritising what the perceived satisfaction will
be at the end is the key.

It can, in some ways, be boiled down to quality over quantity
again, in the same way that true sexual satisfaction comes from a
deep emotional connection rather than how often you have sex.
You might think we would do a better job of appreciating that
concept today, especially with the emphasis on mindfulness and
personal fulfilment in modern culture, but the myth of forever is
so ingrained that we easily forget it. We still cling to the idea that
longevity equals success, rather than focusing on the depth and
quality of the connection we nurture in the present.

The investment model shows that the effort and resources
invested in a relationship significantly predict its longevity and,
more importantly, satisfaction levels.[6] This model emphasises three
factors: satisfaction, quality of alternatives and investment size. The
more you invest – emotionally, mentally and even practically –
the more committed you become to maintaining the relationship.
So, instead of taking for granted that you'll be together forever,
it's actually what you commit to and invest in the relationship
that predicts its success. The model clarifies that satisfaction isn't a
passive outcome but the result of active, ongoing investment.

Every time I'm interviewed, one of the first three questions is,
'How long have you been married?' What they're trying to do is
qualify my ability to talk about relationships based on how long
I've been in mine. No one has ever asked me, 'How satisfied are
you in your relationship?'

I often hear people say that relationships today are not as
strong because they don't last as long as, say, their grandparents'

marriage. What I want to say in response is, 'But how happy were they?' I loved my grandparents, and I don't want to be too hard on them, especially as relationship expectations and standards have changed over time, but I don't think the longevity of their relationship necessarily meant that it was always a happy one. For example, they slept in different rooms, and it wasn't because one of them snored. Over the course of their relationship, they actually divorced and then remarried, so they were together for a long time, and they obviously had a close connection, but I know the satisfaction was not always there. So, we all have to do a better job and stop using longevity as the litmus test of relationship success. The bottom line is that relationship success should be about satisfaction, not how long it lasts.

SELF-GUIDED INTERVENTION: MOVING BEYOND 'FOREVER' AND FOCUSING ON RELATIONSHIP SATISFACTION

OBJECTIVE

To shift your focus from the myth of 'forever' to a more realistic and satisfying approach to relationships that prioritises everyday connection, growth and appreciation over the pursuit of longevity.

INTRODUCTION

The idea that a relationship will last forever is comforting. It gives us a sense of security, a belief that love can withstand anything. However, this notion can be misleading. Believing that a relationship will inevitably last forever can lead to complacency, a lack of growth and the temptation to take our partners for granted. Instead of seeing forever as the marker of success, it's more helpful to view relationship satisfaction as something that's achieved through mutual effort, communication and growth, right now, in the present. This intervention encourages you to reflect on how you can nurture your relationship daily, celebrate small moments of success and continually invest in your partnership, rather than relying on the assumption that it will naturally last a lifetime.

PART I: UNDERSTANDING THE MYTH OF FOREVER

I. RECOGNISE THE FOREVER MYTH

- Do you believe your partner will always be with you, no matter what? How has this belief shaped your engagement in the relationship?
- Many people assume that once they're in a committed relationship, the hard part is over. This can lead to them neglecting the ongoing work a relationship needs. Aiming for forever might cause you to miss out on actively nurturing your connection with your partner.
- Example: 'I assumed that once we got through the early years, the rest would be easy. But over time, I realised we weren't putting the same effort into our relationship any more because we assumed we'd always be together.'

2. THE IMPACT OF THE FOREVER MYTH

- Avoidance of conflict: When we believe a relationship will last forever, we might avoid addressing issues, hoping they will resolve themselves.
- Complacency: Assuming a relationship is unbreakable may lead to putting in less effort, which can create distance and dissatisfaction.
- False sense of security: Assuming a permanent future can prevent us from appreciating our partner's efforts, leading to a lack of gratitude and communication.
- Activity: Reflect on a recent conflict or challenge in your relationship. Did you address it actively or did you hope it would resolve itself? How did that affect your relationship?

- Example: 'When we didn't talk about the things that bothered us, they built up into bigger issues. Once we started communicating regularly, we realised how much we had been avoiding.'

PART 2: SHIFTING FOCUS TO SATISFACTION OVER LONGEVITY

I. FOCUS ON PRESENT SATISFACTION

- A satisfying relationship is one that grows and evolves, not one that merely lasts. Longevity should be a by-product of continuous effort, adaptation and mutual care.
- Ask yourself how satisfied you are in your relationship right now and what you could do to increase that satisfaction, even in small ways.
- Example: 'Once we started checking in with one another more regularly, it helped us to reconnect. Now we make an effort to enjoy small moments, like a quiet breakfast or an evening walk.'

2. PUT IN THE EFFORT AND INVESTMENT

- The more emotional, mental and practical investment you make in your relationship, the more satisfied and committed you will be. The investment model shows that the more you put into your relationship, the stronger your connection becomes.
- Activity: Think of three ways you can invest in your relationship this week, whether it's through kind words, acts of service or spending quality time together.
- Example: 'One small way we invest in our relationship is by leaving each other notes of appreciation. It takes just a minute, but it keeps us connected.'

PART 3: CELEBRATING THE JOURNEY

I. CELEBRATE SMALL WINS

- Instead of waiting for big milestones like anniversaries to celebrate your relationship, start acknowledging the smaller, everyday successes. Celebrate getting through a stressful week, solving a problem together or simply appreciating a kind gesture.

- Activity: Identify a moment this week where you and your partner worked together or supported each other. How can you celebrate that moment?
- Example: 'Every Friday night, we have a glass of wine together and talk about what we've accomplished, both individually and as a couple. It's a simple ritual that brings us closer.'

2. MARK GROWTH, NOT TIME

- While anniversaries are meaningful, the true celebration should be about the growth you've experienced as a couple. Acknowledge the ways you've both adapted, learned and overcome challenges.
- Activity: Reflect on the past year. How have you both grown, either individually or as a couple? What challenges have you faced and what have you learned from them?
- Example: 'We realised that moving to a new city tested our relationship in ways we hadn't anticipated, but it also made us more resilient.'

PART 4: TAKING A NEW APPROACH TO FOREVER

I. REFLECT ON YOUR RELATIONSHIP FOR ACTIVE GROWTH

- Reflection is a powerful tool for maintaining awareness of your relationship's health. Set aside time to reflect on your relationship and write about how you can continue to grow together.
- Activity: Once a month, take ten minutes to reflect on a specific aspect of your relationship. Focus on where you are now, what's working well and what you'd like to improve. Then share your reflections with your partner.
- Example: 'Every month, we sit down and talk about what's been going well and where we can improve. It keeps us both focused on making each other feel valued.'

2. EMBRACE PRESENT EFFORT

- The idea of forever can lead to passive effort, but relationships require active care, attention and nurturing every day. Instead of focusing on the future, focus on the daily practices that keep your relationship strong.
- Activity: Make a list of the daily or weekly practices you can adopt to nurture your relationship, such as scheduling quality time, expressing gratitude or checking in emotionally with one another.
- Example: 'We make a point to check in on how we're feeling emotionally once a week. It's a chance to talk about anything that's been on our minds and strengthen our connection.'

3. NURTURE A BALANCED PERSPECTIVE ON LONGEVITY

- While it's fine to hope for a lasting relationship, understand that longevity isn't the only measure of success. What matters more is how fulfilled and connected you feel throughout the relationship journey.
- Reflect by asking what daily practices help you stay connected to your partner, and how you can use these practices to nurture a healthier relationship.
- Example: 'We stopped focusing on how many years we've been together and started focusing on how happy we are in the present. It's a small shift, but it makes all the difference.'

CONCLUSION

Believing in forever can lead to complacency, whereas a strong relationship is built on daily effort, mutual growth and small, meaningful celebrations. Shift your focus from assuming a long-term guarantee to appreciating the present. By nurturing your relationship each day, through reflection, small celebrations and shared growth, you build a bond that's more likely to thrive — regardless of how long it lasts.

TAKEAWAY

A fulfilling relationship is not guaranteed by longevity alone. Success is measured in the daily efforts you make, the growth you experience and the joy you find together in the present moment.

CONCLUSION

Picking up and reading this book in the first place is a very good indicator that you already had some appreciation of the importance of a healthy, fulfilling relationship on your well-being. It also suggests that you had some level of understanding that love is not something that just happens without effort and commitment. If that was the case, your instincts were correct — as I said at the outset, the simple truth is that relationships take work. Leaning on the information and knowledge I have outlined, and using the self-guided interventions, will provide you with a roadmap to navigate the work required to forge and sustain the relationship that you want and deserve. From conflict resolution strategies to fostering deeper emotional connections, the practical tools I have shared will prepare you to overcome the complexities of keeping love with confidence and compassion.

I can't stress enough how important it is not to fall into the trap of believing the many myths about relationships that we are bombarded with on a daily basis. Those myths are ultimately harmful, and even have the power to sabotage your relationship, which is why it is so important to replace them with truths rooted in research and experience. By focusing on the things that are actually important, you will be able to set healthier, more realistic expectations. For example, true relationship success isn't measured by how long it lasts, but by the depth of fulfilment and mutual satisfaction it brings. By focusing on what truly matters — emotional fitness, shared goals and genuine connection, to name but a few — you will be in a much better position to achieve your highest relationship potential.

Long-lasting love is not a destination but a journey of mutual growth, adaptability and intentional effort. If you embrace love as dynamic and ever-evolving, you will be empowered to build relationships that thrive through life's challenges and changes. Similarly, a fulfilling relationship isn't built in isolation. By embracing self-reliance and cultivating diverse support networks, you can relieve unnecessary pressure on your partnership and benefit from rich connections in all areas of life.

Being in a fulfilling, supportive and loving relationship is the bedrock of my well-being and happiness, and I know it can be for you too. So, let go of the relationship myths that will only hold you back and embark on the journey towards long-lasting love and happiness.

NOTES

INTRODUCTION

1 Orbuch, T.L., Veroff, J. and Hunter, A.G., 'Black couples, white couples: The early years of marriage'. In Hetherington, E.M. (ed.), *Coping with divorce, single parenting, and remarriage: A risk and resiliency perspective* (Lawrence Erlbaum Associates Publishers, 1999).

MYTH I

1 Maslow, A.H., 'A theory of human motivation'. *Psychological Review* 50(4) (1943): 370–96.

2 Amato, P.R., *Alone Together: How Marriage in America Is Changing* (Harvard University Press, 2007).

3 Ibid.

4 'People & Parliament transforming society'. *UK Parliament* (n.d.). https://www.parliament.uk/about/living-heritage/transformingsociety/private-lives/relationships/overview/wedlock-or-deadlock/

5 Willingham, A.J., 'What is no-fault divorce, and why do some conservatives want to get rid of it?' CNN (2023). https://edition.cnn.com/2023/11/27/us/no-fault-divorce-explained-history-wellness-cec/index.html

6 Ortiz-Ospina, E. and Roser, M., 'Marriages and divorces'. *Our World in Data* (2020). https://ourworldindata.org/marriages-and-divorces

7 Orbuch, T.L., Veroff, J. and Hunter, A.G., 'Black couples, white couples: The early years of marriage'. In Hetherington, E.M. (ed.), *Coping with divorce, single parenting, and remarriage: A risk and resiliency perspective* (Lawrence Erlbaum Associates Publishers, 1999).

8 Ryff, C.D. and Singer, B., 'Know thyself and become what you are: A eudaimonic approach to psychological well-being'. *Journal of Happiness Studies* 9(1) (2008): 13–39.

9 Waldinger, R. and Schulz, M., *The Good Life: Lessons from the World's Longest Study on Happiness* (Rider, 2023).

10 Dunbar, R.I.M., 'Neocortex size as a constraint on group size in primates'. *Journal of Human Evolution* 22(6) (1992): 469–93.

11   Granovetter, M.S., 'The strength of weak ties'. *American Journal of Sociology* 78(6) (1973): 1360–80.
12   Finkel, E.J., Hui, C.M., Carswell, K.L. and Larson, G.M., 'The suffocation of marriage: Climbing Mount Maslow without enough oxygen', *Psychological Inquiry* 25(1) (2014), 1–41.

MYTH 2

1   Finkel, E.J., Hui, C.M., Carswell, K.L. and Larson, G.M., 'The suffocation of marriage: Climbing Mount Maslow without enough oxygen'. *Psychological Inquiry* 25(1) (2014): 1–41.
2   Goldman-Wetzler, J., 'Conflict during quarantine is inevitable. How can we deal with it?' *Psychology Today* (18 April 2020).

MYTH 3

1   Gottman, J.M., and Levenson, R.W., 'Marital processes predictive of later dissolution: Behavior, physiology, and health'. *Journal of Personality and Social Psychology,* 63(2) (1992): 221–33.
2   Gottman, J.M. and Silver, N., *The Seven Principles for Making Marriage Work* (Orion Spring, 2018).
3   Huston, T.L., 'What's love got to do with it? Why some marriages succeed and others fail'. *Personal Relationships* 16(3) (2009): 301–27.
4   'Marriage and Cohabitation in the U.S.'. Pew Research Center (2019). https://www.pewresearch.org/social-trends/2019/11/06/marriage-and-cohabitation-in-the-u-s/
5   Hawkins, A.J., Carroll, J.S., Wright Jones, A.M. and James, S.L., 'Capstones vs. Cornerstones: Is Marrying Later Always Better?' *State of Our Unions*, the Wheatley Institution (2022).
6   Meunier, V. and Baker, W., 'Positive couple relationships: The evidence for long-lasting relationship satisfaction and happiness'. In *Positive relationships: Evidence based practice across the world* (Springer Netherlands, 2011).
7   Sternberg, R.J., 'A triangular theory of love'. *Psychological Review* 93(2) (1986): 119–35.
8   Glantz, M.J., Chamberlain, M.C., Liu, Q., Hsieh, C.C., Edwards, K.R., Van Horn, A. and Recht, L. 'Gender disparity in the rate of partner abandonment in patients with serious medical illness'. *Cancer* 15(22) (2009): 5237–42.
9   Carlson, R., *Don't Sweat the Small Stuff: Simple Ways to Keep the Little Things from Overtaking Your Life* (Hodder Paperbacks, 1998).

MYTH 4

1   Rholes, W.S. and Simpson, J.A., *Adult Attachment: Theory, Research, and Clinical Implications* (Guilford Press, 2004).

2   Stanley, S.M., Amato, P.R., Johnson, C.A. and Markman, H.J., 'Premarital education, marital quality, and marital stability: Findings from a large, random household survey'. *Journal of Family Psychology* 20(1) (2006): 117–26; Carroll, J.S. and Doherty, W.J., 'Evaluating the effectiveness of premarital prevention programs: A meta-analytic review of outcome research'. *Family Relations: An Interdisciplinary Journal of Applied Family Studies* 52(2) (2003): 105–18; Fawcett, E.B., Hawkins, A.J., Blanchard, V.L. and Carroll, J.S., 'Do premarital education programs really work? A meta-analytic study'. *Family Relations: An Interdisciplinary Journal of Applied Family Studies* 59(3) (2010): 232–9.

3   Eidell, L., 'Ben Affleck and Jennifer Garner's relationship: A look back'. *People* (26 July 2024). https://people.com/movies/ben-affleck-jennifer-garner-relationship-timeline

4   Jensen, E., 'Jada Pinkett Smith bares all about marriage in interview, book: "Hell of a rugged journey"'. *USA Today* (n.d.). https://eu.usatoday.com/story/entertainment/books/2023/10/16/will-smith-jada-pinkett-smith-marriage-strengthened-after-oscars-slap/71158780007/

MYTH 5

1   Gross, J.J. and John, O.P., 'Individual differences in two emotion regulation processes: Implications for affect, relationships, and well-being'. *Journal of Personality and Social Psychology* 85(2) (2003): 348–62.

2   Rusbult, C.E. and van Lange, P.A.M., 'Interdependence, interaction, and relationships'. *Annual Review of Psychology* 54 (2003): 351–75.

3   Gottman, J.M. and Levenson, R.W., 'Marital processes predictive of later dissolution: Behavior, physiology, and health'. *Journal of Personality and Social Psychology* 63(2) (1992): 221–33.

4   Laurenceau, J.P., Barrett, L.F. and Pietromonaco, P.R., 'Intimacy as an interpersonal process: The importance of self-disclosure, partner disclosure, and perceived partner responsiveness in interpersonal exchanges'. *Journal of Personality and Social Psychology* 74(5) (1998): 1238–51.

5   Karney, B.R. and Bradbury, T.N., 'The longitudinal course of marital quality and stability: A review of theory, method, and research'. *Psychological Bulletin* 118(1) (1995): 3–34.

MYTH 6

1   Muise, A., Schimmack, U. and Impett, E.A., 'Sexual frequency predicts greater well-being, but more is not always better'. *Social Psychological and Personality Science* 7(4) (2016): 295–302.

2   Mark, K., Herbenick, D., Fortenberry, D., Sanders, S. and Reece, M., 'The object of sexual desire: Examining the "what" in "what do you desire?"' *The Journal of Sexual Medicine* 11(11) (2014): 2709–19.

3   Avery-Clark, C. and Weiner, L. *The Wiley Handbook of Sex Therapy* (Wiley Blackwell, 2017), pp. 165–89.

MYTH 7

1   Payne, J.D., Stickgold, R., Swanberg, K. and Kensinger, E.A., 'Sleep preferentially enhances memory for emotional components of scenes'. *Psychological Science* 19(8) (2008): 781–8.
2   Denson, T.F., Capper, M.M., Oaten, M., Friese, M. and Schofield, T.P., 'Self-control training decreases aggression in response to provocation in aggressive individuals'. *Journal of Research in Personality* 45(2) (2011): 252–6.
3   Rogge, R.D. and Bradbury, T.N., 'Till violence does us part: The differing roles of communication and aggression in predicting adverse marital outcomes'. *Journal of Consulting and Clinical Psychology* 67(3) (1999): 340–51.
4   Yoo, S.S., Gujar, N., Hu, P., Jolesz, F.A. and Walker, M.P., 'The human emotional brain without sleep – a prefrontal amygdala disconnect'. *Current Biology* 17(20) (2007): R877–8; Finkel, E.J., Slotter, E.B., Luchies, L.B., Walton, G.M. and Gross, J.J., 'A brief intervention to promote conflict reappraisal preserves marital quality over time'. *Psychological Science* 24(8) (2013): 1595–601.

MYTH 8

1   Brown, A. R. & Manning, W. D., 'Relationship status trends according to age and gender, 2019–2021'. *Family Profiles, FP-21–25*. National Center for Family & Marriage Research (2021).
2   Sassler, S. and Miller, A.J., 'Class differences in cohabitation processes'. *Family Relations* 60(2) (2011): 163–77.
3   Van der Wiel, R., Gillespie, B. J. and Tølbøll, L., 'Migration for co-residence among long-distance couples: The role of local family ties and gender'. Population Space and Place, 29(2) (2022).
4   'The Green Flags Study'. *Tinder Newsroom* (2024). https://www.tinderpressroom.com/The-Green-Flags-Study
5   Dush, C.M.K., Cohan, C.L. and Amato, P.R., 'The relationship between cohabitation and marital quality and stability: Change across cohorts?' *Journal of Marriage and Family*, 65 (2003): 539–49.
6   Kline, G.H., Stanley, S.M., Markman, H.J., Olmos-Gallo, P.A., St. Peters, M., Whitton, S.W. and Prado, L.M. 'Timing Is Everything: Pre-Engagement Cohabitation and Increased Risk for Poor Marital Outcomes'. *Journal of Family Psychology* 18(2) (2004): 311–18.
7   Perelli-Harris, B., Berrington, A., Gassen, N.S., Galezewska, P. and Holland, J.A., 'The rise in divorce and cohabitation: Is there a link?' *Population and Development Review* 43(2) (2017): 303–29.

MYTH 9

1 Roth, G., Vansteenkiste, M. and Ryan, R.M., 'Integrative emotion regulation: Process and development from a self-determination theory perspective'. *Development and Psychopathology* 31(3) (2019): 945–56; Shrestha, P.S., Shaver, S.R., Perlman, T.T. and Walsham, W., 'Emotional dimensions of infidelity: An analysis of psychological and emotional factors affecting relationship infidelity'. *Jurnal Sosial, Sains, Terapan Dan Riset (Sosateris)* 11(2) (2023): 88–103.
2 Mullinax, M., Barnhart, K.J. and Herbenick, D., 'Women's experiences with feelings and attractions for someone outside their primary relationship'. *Journal of Sex & Marital Therapy* 42(5) (2016): 431–47.

MYTH 10

1 'Many couples may share love, but don't share money'. *Policygenius* (2019). https://www.policygenius.com/personal-finance/news/couples-manage-money/
2 'Get engaged over the holiday? It's time to set a date … to talk about money'. *SunTrust Banks* (2019).
3 Bieber, C., 'Revealing divorce statistics in 2024'. *Forbes Advisor* (27 September 2024). https://www.forbes.com/advisor/legal/divorce/divorce-statistics/
4 El Issa, E., '2023 American household credit card debt study'. *NerdWallet* (8 January 2024). https://www.nerdwallet.com/article/credit-cards/average-credit-card-debt-household
5 Vlahakis-Indiana, G., 'Do joint finances make marriages happier?' *Futurity* (5 May 2023). https://www.futurity.org/marriages-money-happiness-relationships-2915282/

MYTH 11

1 'Why women say "I'm sorry" more than men'. *Business Insider* (9 July 2012). https://www.psychologicalscience.org/news/why-women-say-im-sorry-more-than-men.html
2 'NCBI ROFL: Why woman apologize more than men'. *Discover Magazine* (12 October 2011). https://www.discovermagazine.com/the-sciences/ncbi-rofl-why-women-apologize-more-than-men
3 Schumann, K. and Ross, M., 'Why women apologize more than men: Gender differences in thresholds for perceiving offensive behavior'. *Psychological Science* 21(11) (2010): 1649–55.
4 Meunier, V. and Baker, W., 'Positive couple relationships: The evidence for long-lasting relationship satisfaction and happiness'. In: Roffey, S. (ed.), *Positive Relationships* (Springer, 2012).
5 Meuwly, N. and Davila, J., 'Feeling bad when your partner is away: The role of dysfunctional cognition and affect regulation strategies in

insecurely attached individuals'. *Journal of Social and Personal Relationships* 36(1) (2019): 22–42.

6   Ohio State University, 'The 6 Elements of an Effective Apology, According to Science' (12 July 2018). https://news.osu.edu/the-6-elements-of-an-effective-apology-according-to-science/

MYTH 12

1   Sternberg, R.J., 'Construct validation of a triangular love scale'. *European Journal of Social Psychology* 27(3) (1997): 313–35.

2   Acevedo, B.P., Aron, A., Fisher, H.E. and Brown, L.L., 'Neural correlates of long-term intense romantic love'. *Social Cognitive and Affective Neuroscience* 7(2) (2012): 145–59.

3   Finkel, E.J., Hui, C.M., Carswell, K.L. and Larson, G.M., 'The suffocation of marriage: Climbing Mount Maslow without enough oxygen'. *Psychological Inquiry* 25(1) (2014): 1–41.

4   Chapman, G., *The Five Love Languages: How to Express Heartfelt Commitment to Your Mate* (Northfield Publishing, 1992).

5   Benson, K., 'The magic relationship ratio, according to science'. *The Gottman Institute* (18 September 2024). https://www.gottman.com/blog/the-magic-relationship-ratio-according-science/

MYTH 13

1   Waldinger, R. and Schulz, M., *The Good Life: Lessons from the World's Longest Study on Happiness* (Rider, 2023).

2   Henrich, J., *The Weirdest People in the World: How the West Became Psychologically Peculiar and Particularly Prosperous* (Penguin, 2021).

3   Masci, D., 'Shared religious beliefs in marriage important to some, but not all, married Americans'. Pew Research Center (27 October 2016).

4   Gottman, J.M., *Principia amoris: The new science of love* (Routledge, 2014).

5   Kamp Dush, C.M., Taylor, M.G. and Kroeger, R.A., 'Marital Happiness and Psychological Well-Being Across the Life Course'. *Family Relations* 57(2) (2008): 211–26.

6   Jardine, B.B., Vannier, S. and Voyer, D., 'Emotional intelligence and romantic relationship satisfaction: A systematic review and meta-analysis'. *Personality and Individual Differences* 196 (2022).

7   Schoen, R. and Canudas-Romo, V., 'Timing effects on divorce: 20th century experience in the United States'. *Journal of Marriage and Family* 68(3) (2006): 749–58.

8   Diener, E. and Seligman, M.E.P., 'Very happy people'. *Psychological Science* 13(1) (2002): 81–4.

MYTH 14

1   Early Intervention Foundation, 'What does the evidence tell us about the impact of parental conflict on children?' https://reducingparentalconflict. eif.org.uk/child-impact/

MYTH 15

1   Joseph, W. and Bleske-Rechek, A.L., 'Sex Differences in Young Adults' Attraction to Their Opposite-Sex Friends: Natural Sampling Versus Mental Concepts'. University of Wisconsin (2017).

MYTH 16

1   Apostolou, M., Constantinou, C. and Zalaf, A., 'How people react to their partners' infidelity: An explorative study'. *Personal Relationships* 29(4) (2022): 913–32.

2   Leeker, O. and Carlozzi, A. 'Effects of Sex, Sexual Orientation, Infidelity Expectations, and Love on Distress related to Emotional and Sexual Infidelity'. *Journal of Marital & Family Therapy* 40(1) (2014): 68–91.

3   Rokach, A. and Chan, S.H. 'Love and Infidelity: Causes and Consequences'. *International Journal of Environmental Research and Public Health* 20(5) (2023): 3904.

4   Buss, D.M., Larsen, R.J., Westen, D. and Semmelroth, J. 'Sex Differences in Jealousy: Evolution, Physiology, and Psychology'. *Psychological Science* 3(4) (1992): 251–56.

5   Roberts, K., Jaurequi, M., Kimmes, J. and Selice, L., 'Trait Mindfulness and Relationship Satisfaction: The Role of Forgiveness Among Couples'. *Journal of Marital and Family Therapy* 47 (2020).

6   The Gottman Institute. 'Learning to Love Again After an Affair' (2016). https://www.gottman.com/blog/learning-to-love-again-after-an-affair/

MYTH 17

1   Omarzu, J. 'A Disclosure Decision Model: Determining How and When Individuals Will Self-Disclose'. *Personality and Social Psychology Review* 4(2) (2000): 174–85.

2   Vangelisti, A.L. and Young, S.L., 'When words hurt: The effects of perceived intentionality on interpersonal relationships'. *Journal of Social and Personal Relationships* 17(3) (2000): 393–424.

3   Petronio, S. and Altman, I., *Boundaries of Privacy: Dialectics of Disclosure* (State University of New York Press, 2002).

MYTH 18

1   Basson, R. 'The Female Sexual Response: A Different Model'. *Journal of Sex & Marital Therapy* 26(1) (2000): 51–65.

2   Livingstone, K.M. and Isaacowitz, D.M., 'Age and emotion regulation in daily life: Frequency, strategies, tactics, and effectiveness'. *Emotion* 21(1) (2021): 39−51.

3   Gurney, K., *Mind the Gap: The Truth about Desire and How to Futureproof Your Sex Life* (Headline Home, 2020).

MYTH 19

1   Elwert, F. and Christakis, N.A. 'The effect of widowhood on mortality by the causes of death of both spouses'. *American Journal of Public Health* 98(11) (2008): 2092−8.

2   Rees, P., 'The Q Interview: Rick Rubin'. Q (October 2009): 98.

3   Elgaddal, N., Kramarow, E.A. and Reuben, C., 'Physical Activity among Adults Aged 18 and Over: United States, 2020'. Center for Disease Control and Prevention (2022).

4   Anderson, G.O. and Thayer, C. 'Loneliness and Social Connections: A National Survey of Adults 45 and Older'. AARP (14 September 2008). https://www.aarp.org/pri/topics/social-leisure/relationships/loneliness-social-connections/

5   Mehl, M.R., Vazire, S., Holleran, S.E. and Clark, S.C., 'Eavesdropping on Happiness: Well-being is Related to Having Less Small Talk and More Substantive Conversations'. *Psychological Science* 21(4) (2010): 539−41.

6   Ryan, R.M. and Deci, E.L. 'Self-Determination Theory and the Facilitation of Intrinsic Motivation, Social Development, and Well-Being'. *American Psychologist* 55(1) (2000): 68−78.

7   Berkman, L.F. and Glass, T.A. 'Social Integration, Social Networks, Social Support, and Health'. In Berkman, L.F. and Kawachi, I. (eds), *Social Epidemiology* (Oxford University Press, 2000).

8   Ibid.

MYTH 20

1   Lee, S.W.S and Schwarz, N., 'Framing love: When it hurts to think we were made for each other'. *Journal of Experimental Social Psychology* 54 (2014): 61−67.

2   Knee, C.R., 'Implicit theories of relationships: Assessment and prediction of romantic relationship initiation, coping, and longevity'. *Journal of Personality and Social Psychology* 74(2) (1998): 360−70.

3   Vannier, S.A. and O'Sullivan, L.F., 'Passion, connection, and destiny: How romantic expectations help predict satisfaction and commitment in young adults' dating relationships'. *Journal of Social and Personal Relationships* 34(2) (2017): 235−57.

4   Dweck, C.S., *Mindset: Changing the Way You Think to Fulfil Your Potential* (Robinson, 2017).

MYTH 2I

1   Bächtold-Stäubli, H., *Folklore Suisse* (Schweizerische Gesellschaft für Volkskunde, 1921).

2   Lee, C., *Wedding Anniversaries: From Paper to Diamond* (Ryland Peters & Small, 2001).

3   Halonen Bratcher, E., 'Exchange these traditional wedding vows at your Hindu ceremony'. *The Knot* (15 December 2021). https://www.theknot.com/content/hindu-wedding-vow

4   Levey, J., 'Muslim wedding vows inspired by Quran verses on love and marriage'. *American Marriage Ministries* (7 November 2022). https://theamm.org/articles/1440-muslim-wedding-vows-inspired-by-quran-verses-on-love-marriage

5   Gable, S.L. and Reis, H.T., 'Good news! Capitalizing on positive events in an interpersonal context'. In: Zanna, M.P. (ed.), *Advances in Experimental Social Psychology*, Vol. 42 (Academic Press, 2010), pp. 195–257.

6   Rusbult, C.E., Martz, J.M. and Agnew, C.R., 'The Investment Model Scale: Measuring commitment level, satisfaction level, quality of alternatives, and investment size'. *Personal Relationships*, 5(4) (1998): 357–91.

ABOUT THE AUTHOR

Photograph © Christopher Bethell

Paul Carrick Brunson is a globally acclaimed relationship expert, matchmaker, television host and entrepreneur based in London. He currently co-hosts *Married at First Sight UK* and *Celebs Go Dating*, where his insights into relationship science reach millions. As the Global Relationship Insights Expert for Tinder, he's deeply involved in shaping the future of digital dating.

Paul also hosts the #1 *We Need to Talk* podcast, a platform that delivers raw, insightful discussions on relationships, personal growth and societal impact. It's become a destination for those seeking thought-provoking and transformative conversations.

Beyond his broadcasting work, Paul is a proud co-owner of Sutton United FC, where he's committed to building a diverse and inclusive community through the club. A dedicated philanthropist, he founded Give Love Build Hope, a non-profit focused on transforming schools in the Caribbean. A proud second-generation Jamaican, Paul's greatest joy comes from his roles as a husband and father.